COACHING THE
NO-HUDDLE
OFFENSE

G. MARK McELROY

COACHES CHOICE

www.coacheschoice.com

ISBN: 1-58518-210-9
Library of Congress Catalog Card Number: 97-81208

Book layout and cover design: Paul Lewis
Front cover photo: Courtesy of Allen's Studio

Coaches Choice
PO Box 1828
Monterey, CA 93942

This book is dedicated to my Lord and Savior Jesus Christ from whom "all things are possible." To my wife, Deanne, who on a daily basis continues to exhibit love, courage, and support in the midst of difficult circumstances. To my energetic children, Seth, Caleb, Hannah, and Grace, who always provide me with unconditional love and wonderful experiences; and to my loving parents, George and Carolyn, who have always been a shining example of Christianity.

All outstanding football programs are built upon the hard work, pride, and loyalty of many people. The San Clemente Football program was built with strong administrative support, selfless parental support, incredible coaches, and committed football players. Our success can be directly attributed to all of these people.

When implementing a new offense, much investigation must occur. Many coaches have impacted my thought on offensive football. I have asked questions of every successful coach with whom I have come in contact. I would like to thank all of the coaches who have influenced my thought on football over the years through personal friendships and those who have simply taken the time to engage in conversation. Additionally, I have watched videos, been to clinics, visited universities, and read many articles and outstanding books by great coaches that continue to have an impact on my offensive thought. I would like to thank all of the coaches who have opened up their wealth of knowledge to me through all of these methods. I am especially grateful to the following men who were instrumental in my No-Huddle investigation: Steve Crapo, Mike Milner, Eric Patton, Eric Johnson, Tom Smythe, Trent Dilfer, Dan Morrison, Mark Speckman and many other coaches too numerous to mention. I would continue to encourage coaches to share information with each other to keep coaches like myself pursuing the cutting edge of this sport that we all love so dearly.

I will never be able to repay LaVell Edwards for the opportunity he gave me to coach for him in 1988 and 1989. My experience at BYU changed my life professionally as an educator and as a football coach. My understanding of offensive football is grounded in the BYU offensive scheme. I learned a great deal from a technical and schematic standpoint from the great coaches at BYU. As an indicator of their greatness, Norm Chow, Roger French, Lance Reynolds, and Chris Pella continue to produce outstanding offenses every year at BYU that rank in the top five nationally.

Several coaches have influenced my thoughts on the No-Huddle offense; however, the two coaches who had the most influence on my No-Huddle thought were Bill Cunerty, the head football coach at Saddleback College (1984 and 1996 National Junior College Champions) and Tom Craft (former offensive coordinator at San Diego State and current head football coach at Palomar College, 1991 and 1993 National Junior College Champions). Bill is one of the most creative offensive coaches that I have ever met and Tom is one of the brightest coaches to whom I have ever listened. To these men, I am greatly indebted for their knowledge and their continued willingness to share information about offensive football.

This book was put together with the help of a couple of very special people. I would like to thank Dr. Fowle for providing expert assistance in photo editing, and I am especially grateful for Jon Hamro and his unique perspective on offensive football and his unselfish willingness to help edit this book.

Finally, your system is only as strong as those within it. The players at San Clemente High School over the past three years have really made this style effective. In addition to great athletes, I also feel that I have a great football staff. Our staff members support each other through good times and bad and are very good friends. Without the support, effort, camaraderie and professionalism of this staff, our offensive success would be greatly diminished. Steve Crapo has been a tremendous influence on my life both personally and professionally, and I cherish his close friendship. I am deeply indebted to the collective efforts and unselfish support of the following varsity coaches and the rest of the football staff at San Clemente High School: Brad Budde, Bob Burges, Steve Crapo, Bill Everhart, Jon Hamro, Dan Johnson, and Rod Cummings.

CONTENTS

I have known Mark McElroy for many years, ever since he coached football at BYU while he was completing his doctorate degree in sport leadership. He has an excellent football mind and has been an avid student of the game over the years. I am delighted that he has decided to share his skill and expertise with his peers through this book.

The No-Huddle offense is an exciting, powerful weapon for a football game. We have found the No-Huddle to be an effective way to put pressure on the defense, creating difficulty in the opponent making easy adjustments or substitutions. It would be rare for a coach to use it as his standard offensive format, but it is a great way to catch the defense off guard and change or maintain the momentum of the game.

Interest in the No-Huddle is high throughout the country, but many coaches don't yet know how to implement it into their game plans. Within this book, Mark demonstrates the "Why, Where, and How" of using this offense. Most importantly, he shows how it can be adapted to any offensive style, making it a feasible weapon for any program.

I believe that coaches at every level will enjoy this book and that it can give them the knowledge and understanding needed to implement the No-Huddle offense into their own schemes. It's an exciting, innovative tool for both coaches and players to use.

LaVell Edwards
Head Football Coach
Brigham Young University

The No-Huddle Offense is an exciting and productive style of offense. It can be adapted to virtually any type of offensive scheme. However, the No-Huddle style and communication can not replace a sound offensive system that is prepared diligently and executed flawlessly. Therefore, it should be made clear that the No-Huddle style discussed in this book is designed to enhance any system of offense a coach is currently employing. This book will discuss the advantages and disadvantages behind the No-Huddle style and how to maximize the former and minimize the latter, as well as provide an in-depth look at installing the communication system, practicing this style of offense, and game night execution. The No-Huddle style coupled with your offensive scheme will enhance your offensive advantage and improve your offensive production dramatically.

Many people believe that the No-Huddle is too difficult to teach at the high school level. This style of offense can and has been run at the high school level very successfully. High school athletes are very capable of learning and executing a No-Huddle offense. This book is aimed at providing the high school coach with the necessary tools to build a No-Huddle system with his current offensive scheme. All good information can transcend disciplines and levels of competition; however, this book is primarily designed to improve offensive football at the high school level.

I began coaching in 1983, on the defensive side of the ball at the high school level. During those early years, I read everything I could find about football and went to every possible clinic in our area. I even traveled across the country to go to many university coaching clinics because of my unquenched thirst for knowledge. I remember seeing Eddie Robinson (Grambling) at an AFCA clinic, sitting in the front row with a notebook and pen in his hand trying to soak up some new knowledge about defensive line play. He provided me with a glimpse into one of the things that makes a great coach: the continual search for knowledge and better ways to coach the game of football. I figured that if a legendary coach of over 40 years was trying to learn something new, then I must always be open to a continual search for new ideas.

After coaching defensive backs, linebackers and quarterbacks for five years at the high school level, I was given a great opportunity to coach football at BYU. It was at BYU that I learned how the football can be thrown on a consistent and successful basis. After my stint at BYU, I had the opportunity to coach the defensive secondary at Whitworth College in Spokane, Washington. These coaching opportunities helped me understand that my family priorities were extremely important and I decided to move back "home" to San Clemente and coach high school football. I am entering my sixth season as the head football coach at San Clemente High School.

The season prior to our league championship in 1995, we were struggling to find a way for our football team to compete and we went to the No-Huddle style out of desperation. We had lost many of our starters and it looked like our team was going to be very weak. We play in the South Coast League in CIF Division I in California (the most difficult division in the state) and our most difficult league opponent, Mater Dei, won the USA Today National Championship that year, as well as in 1996. The No-Huddle style coupled with a four-wide receiver offense seemed to be our chance to be competitive. We had typically been slower and less talented than most of our opponents, so we had to find an advantage. The No-Huddle gave us the edge that we needed.

In the beginning we made numerous mistakes. The transition to this style of offense was difficult, yet challenging and very exciting. We watched several videos by the Buffalo Bills, Sam Wyche, Florida State and Tom Craft from San Diego State University. Our staff also visited San Diego State (they ran the No-Huddle at the time) and attended several No-Huddle clinics. These clinics and videos were informative, but not detailed enough to help us completely develop our system. No books were available on the No-Huddle, so we talked to every coach we knew who had attempted this type of offense. Many coaches offered us sound advice on how to run and install the No-Huddle; however, we found that there were as many ways to run the No-Huddle as there were different types of offenses. Our investigation into this style brought us to a fork in the road in which we had to decide which style to use. We decided to use a combination of styles largely influenced by Bill Cunerty and Tom Craft and developed our own method of No-Huddle. In this book, we will take an in-depth look at the various communication systems and No-Huddle styles that we were introduced to and explore in depth the system that we have developed and use effectively.

No-Huddle offense is not a trendy fly-by-night style of offense, but rather a proven, successful way to upgrade any offensive system. You must first believe in your offensive system and then apply this style in order to have a major advantage over opposing defenses. In 1994, it was purely coincidental that we changed our offensive system at the same time we changed our style to No-Huddle. With my coaching background at BYU, our offense had been primarily two-back with multiple formations, throwing the football approximately 60 percent of the time. However, in 1994, we decided to run a four-wide receiver offense coupled with the No-Huddle out of desperation, because we only had one running back and numerous receivers. In high school, we have discovered that the longest lines of personnel in freshman football are the receivers, so they are much easier to find and replace than a good running back. Running backs are a rare commodity, and therefore we have decided to stick with a single back offense, unless somehow we end up with several great running backs in our program at the same time.

This type of offensive scheme and style places pressure on the quarterback; therefore, your quarterback must have a great mind and a love for the game of football. The single-back offense coupled with the No-Huddle system has allowed us to simplify our pass protection principles and identify fronts and coverages with greater ease. The No-Huddle style can be adapted to the Wing-T, wishbone, single-back, two-back or virtually any other offensive system. It has made our offensive system more effective and it can do the same for yours if you approach it with openness and enthusiasm. Whatever offensive scheme you employ, you must believe in it and get your staff and players to believe and have confidence in it.

The main objective of offensive football is to score as many points as possible to help your team win the football game. The purpose of this book is to introduce you to a style of football that will enable you to maximize your offensive potential, while continuing to run the offensive scheme that you are most confident in. This book will give you the knowledge that will help you improve your current offensive system and/or stimulate thought to pursue another offensive system. In either case, the offensive system can be coupled with the No-Huddle style for a major offensive advantage.

PART 1

COMMUNICATION SYSTEMS

A system of communicating the offense to players is imperative for the No-Huddle style to be successful. In researching the No-Huddle style, many different communication systems were identified. However, five different systems stood out because they were unique, creative, and successful based on the offensive success in programs ranging from the high school level to the NFL. Each system would be interesting to discuss; however, only three systems will be explained in depth. The teams running each system will not be identified to maintain offensive integrity, but the systems will be thoroughly explained so the ideas can help a coaching staff develop their own style of No-Huddle communication.

One of the major questions asked about the No-Huddle system is "How much of the offense should be No-Huddle?" A couple schools of thought exist regarding this issue. When this No-Huddle investigation commenced, several of the high school coaches who were addressed believed that the No-Huddle should only be a part of the offense, because it would be too confusing for the players to learn an entire communication system. At the college level, Tom Craft (offensive coordinator, San Diego State, 1994-1996) believed that a team needed to commit the entire offense to the No-Huddle style in order to be successful. Finally, in the NFL, others believe it is difficult to run the No-Huddle because of personnel trading from team to team. Whatever the philosophy may be for any given team regarding the amount of No-Huddle used, one factor remains constant in successful offensive football: the importance of scheme execution. If the No-Huddle takes time and repetitions away from offensive execution, then the No-Huddle style should be reconsidered or revamped. On the other hand, at San Clemente High School, repetitions have nearly doubled in practice and therefore, offensive scheme execution has improved. The No-Huddle style should not take time away from teaching the correct offensive scheme techniques and principles. The No-Huddle is a time saver and not a time waster. The systems that will be discussed in the following chapters are completely committed to the No-Huddle scheme and their communication is designed for the entire offense.

After careful research into various No-Huddle styles, it became obvious that just like communication in personal relationships, every team has its own style and way of creating dialogue among its members. In the same way that relationship communication varies, team offensive communication is unique to those within the system. Therefore, communication among members of the staff and offensive personnel must fit the personalities of those implementing it.

In traveling around the world, one begins to understand that many languages are spoken. Visiting another country without an understanding of the language can be very frustrating and difficult. Playing defense against a No-Huddle team should be like traveling to a foreign country with absolutely no idea of how to speak the language. The offense can speak fluently to one another with ease while the defense should have no idea of what is being said. Therefore, the No-Huddle "language" should be easy enough for the offense to communicate freely with one another, yet complicated enough to completely confuse the defense.

The No-Huddle styles that will be explored in Part I have completely different terminology, signals, philosophies, and methods. No one style is better than the other. The styles presented in this part are run at the three top levels of football: high school, college, and the NFL. A method exists behind each coach's "madness" on how he communicates with other coaches and the players. If a normal lay person listened to football coaches talk about what coaches consider "normal" football language, they would think that the coaches were from another planet. The styles presented in this section should be used to stimulate thought on how to devise a unique No-Huddle style of communication for any offensive scheme. These systems are currently in use successfully and should be seriously considered when establishing thoughts on developing a No-Huddle system of communication.

Each system of No-Huddle has its own unique style, but they all must communicate the same basic information to the offense. The following items need to be communicated in virtually every offense and will be addressed in each of the following chapters on communication systems:

→ Personnel (positions)
→ Formations
→ Motion (if any)
→ Cadence
→ Live signals and dummy signals
→ Pass plays
→ Play/Action
→ Screens/Specials
→ Pass protection and line calls
→ Offensive holes
→ Running game
→ Audibles and check-with-me system
→ Other special features
→ Evaluation

CHAPTER 1

WHY RUN THE NO-HUDDLE?

The purpose of a huddle is to develop offensive team cohesiveness, discipline, and leadership and to communicate the play to the offensive team. Why would a coach want to disrupt this very important facet of offensive football? One of the main reasons to eliminate the huddle is because it reduces the defense's ability to communicate after plays, which can also disrupt their team cohesiveness, discipline and leadership. Additionally, the defenders can not feed off of one another's emotional energy during the game, which is a major advantage to the offense. The No-Huddle offense can still communicate the offensive play in an effective and expeditious manner. This style can disrupt the natural rhythm of the game that the defense is accustomed to playing, thus giving the offense the advantage in tempo and rhythm. When does No-Huddling disrupt the offensive team's cohesiveness, discipline and leadership? Hopefully never. The offensive team becomes accustomed to its new style and personality and enjoys the freedom associated with the No-Huddle; however, the coach who needs structure in his offense may struggle at first with this new offensive freedom. The fundamental advantages of the No-Huddle offense can give an undermanned team the chance to level the playing field against a difficult opponent.

Offensive coaches are always looking for a way to gain an advantage over the defense. The No-Huddle system provides many unique advantages. These advantages are clearly evidenced by our progressive successes offensively over the past three years as shown in Figure 1-1.

In addition to our offensive successes, this style of offense has increased the average number of plays run in a game by over 33 percent. Figure 1-2 demonstrates how the No-Huddle has increased the number of plays for a 48-minute high school football game. This increase can have a dramatic effect on teams that are used to fewer plays per game. The number of plays can fatigue two-way players much more quickly and force teams that one-platoon to adjust their game plan accordingly.

TEAM STATISTICS

	Pts. Per Game	Total Yds	Passing	Rushing	1st Downs	3rd Down Conv.	Run/Pass Ratio
1993	25	3227	1353	1874	133	43%	62/38
No-Huddle Offense							
1995	30	4045	2666	1379	175	59%	48/52
1996	33	4077	2528	1549	178	57%	47/53

INDIVIDUAL STATISTICS

	Att.	Comp.	Pct.	Yds	TD	Int	Yds/Att.	# of 22 yd + Passing Games
'93 Geoff Buffum	187	89	47.6%	1226	12	6	6.6	1
No-Huddle Offense								
'95 Chris Boden	320	188	58.8%	2592	22	15	8.1	9
'96 Chris Hayward	299	189	63.2%	2527	21	8	8.5	9

Note: In 1995 and 1996 San Clemente had a 1,000 yard receiver and a 1,000 yard rusher each year.

Figure 1-1: A typical 10-game high school football season.

```
Pre-No-Huddle Style
1993     44.2 plays per game

No-Huddle Style
1995     58.7 plays per game
1996     63.9 plays per game
33% increase in average number of plays per game
```

Figure 1-2: Number of average plays per game for San Clemente High School.

Running a No-Huddle offense has many advantages. A brief list of these advantages, many of which will be discussed further in later chapters, includes the following:

→ **Creates Defensive Anxiety:**

⇒ The fast pace increases defensive anxiety levels tremendously.

⇒ Coaches and players are not used to the rhythm of the game.

⇒ Confusion often occurs during "up tempo."

⇒ Difficulty simulating No-Huddle in practice.

⇒ Decreased defensive team communication and unity.

⇒ Opposing coaches must prepare for the added dimension to your offensive scheme.

⇒ Offense dictates the defense (i.e., defense stays in base fronts and coverages).

⇒ Limits defensive substitutions.

⇒ Limits defensive dogs and blitzes.

⇒ Offense controls the tempo of the game.

→ **The Coach Controls the Tempo:** (Three main tempos to keep defenses off balance and confused)

⇒ Slow tempo.

⇒ Regular tempo.

⇒ Up tempo.

→ **Fun to Watch and Play:**

⇒ Spectators enjoy the fast-paced game.

⇒ Easy for anybody to learn.

⇒ Players feel superior with their "secret language."

⇒ Players increase ownership with term/signal inventions.

⇒ Players must pay closer attention in practice for better retention.

⇒ Practice is fun and fast-paced (offensive repetitions nearly double).

⇒ Snap-count and play memory loss are reduced considerably.

⇒ Two-minute offense is standard (no anxiety on offense).

⇒ More plays = more offense = more points.

→ **Conditioning:**

⇒ 33% more plays = 33% more game on both sides of the ball.

⇒ No-Huddle team is used to the longer game.

⇒ Practices are laced with intense conditioning periods.

⇒ Nobody has to run back and forth from the huddle.

⇒ Many teams fatigue during the fourth quarter.

⇒ Opponent's two-way players fatigue more quickly and must be used differently.

⇒ No-Huddle two-way players are used to the lengthy game.

⇒ Passing offenses fatigue defensive linemen very quickly.

Some disadvantages do occur when running the No-Huddle offense. The following reasons might deter a coach from implementing this style of offense:

→ Your defensive coaches may not want the possibility of more plays in a game to defend.

→ Practice organization is less structured.

→ Offensive team cohesive communication (huddle) can suffer.

→ If a team is poor, an increase in plays can mean a bigger loss.

→ Team emphasis could be focused on the No-Huddle offense.

→ Could result in memory overload for two-way players.

In order to run the No-Huddle offense, the entire staff must believe in its potential for success. This style of offense will have an impact on the team's personality, practice organization, and defensive statistical success. Therefore, it is imperative that the defensive staff "buy in" to this style of offense before proceeding.

The main goal of a defense is to limit the number of points scored by the opposing team. As mentioned previously, a football game is generally increased by as much as 33 percent when using the No-Huddle style. Due to the No-Huddle, the opposing offense will have approximately ten to fifteen more plays to score points. Most defensive coaches pride themselves on such game statistics as points scored, total yards, passing and rushing yards, number of first downs, etc. Because the game is increased by the No-Huddle, these "defensive yardsticks" become inflated and are not realistic when compared to those of other teams. A No-Huddle team will run between 25 and 33 percent more plays and have that many more plays run against them in a given season, thus skewing any positive game and season defensive statistics. The defensive staff must be made aware of this change and be willing to sacrifice their own statistical significance in the best interest of the team advantage that is acquired by using the No-Huddle offense.

The defensive staff must also know the No-Huddle style affects many aspects of team preparation, personnel decisions, and game management. Practice tempo and organization are dramatically affected by this style (Chapter Seven). The No-Huddle style lends itself to quick transitions. The offense may score very quickly or be "three and out," forcing the defense back onto the field without much rest. In the No-Huddle style, spectators tend to focus on the success of the offense and give little attention to the defense. The defense must be comfortable with receiving less attention than the offense and feel good about being considered "unsung heroes." With all of these factors in mind, the entire staff must weigh the advantages and the disadvantages of adapting the No-Huddle style to their offensive scheme.

The No-Huddle style affects opposing defenses in many ways. When I was discussing the No-Huddle with defensive coordinators, they shared some of the things that caused them the most problems. Many of these coaches felt that the offense was very difficult to simulate in practice. Some coaches have used two scout teams at a time to try to simulate the speed of the No-Huddle style. When the opponent prepares for the No-Huddle, it is difficult to make scout team adjustments and maintain the practice tempo. These practice adjustments require considerable time to develop, implement, and run. The No-Huddle is an extra component to prepare for and it takes considerable time away from a defense's preparation for the offensive scheme.

Defensive coaches have difficulty on game night. The fast pace increases players' and coaches' anxiety levels, which can result in more defensive mental mistakes. Communication among the defensive players and with the coaches can become rushed and cause confusion. For example, in our first game of 1996, our quarterback ran a sneak for 80 yards while the opposing defense was still trying to get its defensive signal from the coach. Five of the playside players, including the free safety, were still looking at the coach when our quarterback ran by them. Even when things go right for an opposing defense, they are not allowed to huddle and feed on one another's emotions, so the No-Huddle helps destroy defensive team unity.

The defense will often stay in base fronts and coverages for fear of being caught out of position in a fast-paced attack. Facing only base fronts and/or coverages can help reduce offensive preparation time. With all of these things in mind, the advantages of the No-Huddle style become clear.

You are probably reading this book to try to gain an advantage offensively. Many advantages and disadvantages have been discussed regarding this style of offense. It should be quite apparent that the advantages far outweigh the disadvantages. Why doesn't everybody run the No-Huddle? With any style of offense, a coach must feel confident and comfortable teaching, coaching and making any necessary adjustments to the offense his team is using. Some coaches may feel uncomfortable with this style because of the many variables involved, the need to change their practice structure and organization, and a belief that it does not give them enough of an advantage. However, it has been well worth the risk for San Clemente High School. The Air Force Academy runs the triple option in a conference full of single-back and pass-happy schools, and thus gains an advantage by executing an offense that is rarely seen by opposing defenses. The No-Huddle also forces other teams to prepare for a dimension of offense that they do not see very often.

Most coaches are looking for the offensive equalizer. The No-Huddle is it. Most offensive coaches try to dream up ways to keep defensive coordinators up late at night viewing film or stopping certain offensive schemes. If you like to outsmart your opponent with schemes, try adding the No-Huddle to your already crafty scheme and gain a major advantage over the defense. This style can help elevate an undermanned team or help lift a talented team to the next level.

MEMORY LINK SYSTEM

Many memory experts believe picture words, hand signals that imitate those picture words, and the linking of those terms are collectively the most effective way to memorize things. Each term must be remembered in as many of the senses as possible. The players should be able to feel, hear, smell, taste, and see the terms that represent each play. The memory link system employs this methodology to improve retention of offensive schemes. This system is virtually number free and only uses terms to communicate. In many cases these terms are thematic, or "linked" to each other, or are products of outlandish stories surrounding the original term. The more zany and graphic the story about the term, the greater the retention of the information. The following story illustrates this point.

A story was once told about a purple hippo that had really long pink legs. The long pink legs had black spots on them that contracted and expanded when the hippo was very hungry. This hippo had two heads, one completely red with no hair and the other a normal gray color, also with no hair. The hippo was very fast and liked to eat butterflies for food.

This story could probably be easily remembered because of its outlandish nature. Do you remember the color of the hippo's legs? What happens to the hippo's legs when he is hungry? Does the hippo have any hair on his head(s)? The story is the basis for a memory link and, consequently, high retention of offensive terminology. It is used as the springboard for developing the play called "Hippo." Hippo Orange is a pass pattern in this unique memory link system.

PERSONNEL

The eligible personnel are given names that are very similar to those in most offenses: Zeke (Z), Exxon (X), Yankee (Y), Tom (Tailback), and Frank (Fullback). The names are used to make route adjustments and tag receivers for pass read progression adjustments. Personnel groups are also used in this system. They are given animal names: Rhino (two-tight end, two-back); Cheetah (four-wide receiver, single-back); and Eagle (three-wide receiver, two-back). The personnel groups are signaled and yelled from the sideline for a smooth personnel transition on the field before the formation and play are signaled in to the quarterback. Personnel groups and substitutions can be run in Slow or Regular tempo No-Huddle, but not in Up tempo No-Huddle (Chapter Nine).

FORMATIONS

Formations are named like any other offense would name them and signaled in accordingly. An I Right is called "I Right." This system does not conceal the formation terms and signals because the defense would see the formation in a second anyway, formations and motions do not need to be concealed with terminology and signals. In some extreme cases, where the offense has severe formation tendencies, special consideration should be given to concealing formations from the defense as long as possible. Some defenses are designed against formation play tendencies. Therefore, a coach should make every effort to identify the strengths and weaknesses in the offense and use the No-Huddle to accentuate the strengths and cover up the weaknesses.

MOTIONS

This system uses common motion terms that are communicated with the formation when signaled. The terms are common to most teams. For example, Zeke (Z) motions are called Zoom, Zip, Zap, Zorro, etc. The formation is signaled and the motion man will go in motion from his place in the formation called; however, the team that employs this No-Huddle system uses very little motion.

CADENCE

This system values cadence selection very highly. It has at least a dozen ways to call the cadence. The cadence is based upon themes and progressions. In Table 2-1, three different cadence themes are listed. The first theme, NBA centers, is based upon the number of syllables in the center's name, with one-syllable names (Shaq) on one, two-syllable names (Ewing) on two, etc. The second theme is based upon a saying, but the number of letters in the word constitutes the cadence. The third theme is based upon major cities in the United States. The alphabetical progression of the first letter of the city's name determines the snap

	SNAP COUNT			
THEME	**1**	**2**	**3**	**4**
NBA Centers (number of syllables)	Shaq	Ewing	Robinson	Olajuwon
Famous Saying (number of letters in each word)	A	Bo	Can	Do it
US Cities (alphabetical order)	Atlanta	Boston	Cleveland	Detroit

Table 2-1: Memory link system snap counts.

count (A-1, B-2, C-3). These are just a few ways that the snap count can be called. Once the snap count has been determined, the cadence goes "down, set, hut, hut, hut."

LIVE SIGNALS AND DUMMY SIGNALS

Signals are communicated by three people, one having the "live" signal and two having "dummy" signals. The coach stands next to the signal callers and dictates the play to them. The plays are signaled in according to what the play is called. For example, a counter trey is signaled in with a signal representing the counter and not by the litany of code names associated with the counter. The quarterback then calls the play according to any of the code words associated with the counter trey. The quarterback can use any dummy calls and/or non-verbal signals to receivers to confuse the defense. He will use non-verbal signals to receivers on every down whether the signals mean something or not. For example, after the play has been yelled at the line of scrimmage, the quarterback may look both ways and tap the top of his helmet vigorously to signify some sort of non-verbal signal. At the line of scrimmage, the quarterback will say at least three words: a color, one code word or more, possibly a dummy term and the snap count. For example, the play signaled in is Freeze Option right. At the line of scrimmage, the quarterback yells, "Red Ford Shaq." Red stands for the play to go right, Ford is the freeze option, and the ball is snapped on one (Shaq).

PASS PLAYS

Passing plays are given code words that represent the entire pattern. For example, a smash concept pattern is given the code name "Hammer." With this one word, the entire pattern is described to all of the receivers. The protection is called by the color just before the code word. The colors used in determining pass protection direction must have an "l" or "r" in them. For example, Black means to slide the protection left and Brown means to slide the protection right. Therefore, if the call at the line of scrimmage was Black Hammer Shaq, the play would be a smash concept pattern with the protection slid to the left and the ball snapped on one. If this play was called often, alternate terms would have to be invented for the term "Hammer." This change is made through memory linking other like terms associated with a hammer. For example, a hammer is a tool, so all tools could mean the same play: wrench, ratchet, (screw) driver, nail, etc. The same play could also be called Black Nail Shaq. Initially, to come up with the code word "Hammer," a crazy story is told about a talking hammer that lived in Beverly Hills, etc.

Any route adjustment or deviation from the pass pattern must be tagged with the receiver's name and the route adjustment term. For example, Black Nail Zeke Shaq is the same play as Black Hammer Shaq, except Zeke was tagged, telling the quarterback to take a "peek" at the Z receiver before going to his normal read progression. The quarterback can also use non-verbal signals to inform receivers of route adjustments that need to be made. A team with many route adjustment terms could have a difficult time retaining all of the information necessary to run this style of offense.

PLAY/ACTION

Play/action passing is called similar to a basic pass play. A code word such as "Pool" is used to represent a play/action pass. "Pool" is combined with the action of the run to represent the play/action pass with the protection built into the run action fake. The pattern term is included after the run call. For example, the call might be Pool Phone Hammer Shaq. This call means that the play/action will be off a *Phone* run action and the pass pattern will be a *Hammer* on one. The Phone action provides the necessary information for pass protection responsibilities.

SCREENS/SPECIALS

This aspect of the offense is run in the same way as the play/action pass, with code words representing screen passes and specials. Dummy terms and signals can help conceal these plays. Many teams will have associated code words starting with an "l" or "r" to represent certain passes, screens, or specials. For example, the terms "Rocket" and "Lazer" are used for quick screens to the right and left, respectively.

PASS PROTECTION AND LINE CALLS

Pass protection is called by the color preceding the pass pattern call. For example, Black Nail means that the offensive line slides protection to the left because "Black" has an "l" in the name. If the protection called is inappropriate at the line of scrimmage, the quarterback and/or the center can make pass protection adjustments. The line calls are normal calls that are present in a typical offensive system. The quarterback may use code words such as "smart" and "chief" in order to get maximum protection. These words are names of characters from the 1960's comedy *Get Smart*, whose main character was named "Max" (thus, maximum). Line calls and pass protection are practiced daily and protection adjustments are built into the passing scheme.

OFFENSIVE HOLES

Since this system is number-free, hole numbering is inappropriate. The run play concept is taught without the hole numbering system. The defensive front must be learned with all of its important details, but the offensive holes are taught in conceptual offensive plays. For example, the offense understands that the inside zone is run over the guard's outside hip rather than to the one or two hole.

RUNNING GAME

The entire offense is responsible for learning all of the code words for the run game. These code words are completely different from the passing game. The running game uses code words to describe the running play. Prior to the code word being called, a color is called which tells the direction of the play to be run. Any color with an "r" in it tells the offense to run the play to the right. Any color with an "l" in it tells the offense that the run play is going to the left. Runs could be categorized into groups of cars. If a code word for an outside zone run was "Honda," then the play might be called Brown Honda Bo (see Diagram 2-1), which means the Honda play is being run to the right on two. If the defensive line stems or the linebackers move before the snap of the ball, then the quarterback could yell "Oscar" (see Diagram 2-2), which tells the offense to run the same play to the direction opposite the original call.

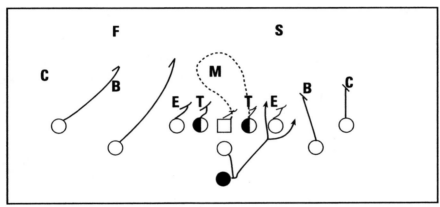

Diagram 2-1: Brown Honda Bo—outside zone (Honda) to the right (Brown) on two (Bo).

AUDIBLES AND CHECK-WITH-ME'S

Audibles can be and are used in this system of No-Huddle. As discussed above, if a run call is made but the play needs to be run the other way, "Oscar" is yelled at the line of scrimmage to change the call. This system can be used as a check-with-me if the call was initially made to one side. Otherwise, a check-with-me play would be called after the quarterback has seen the defensive indicator(s) that determines the play and/or direction of the play. Audibles can also be used to get out of a bad play selection. For example, "Elvis" or anything associated with Elvis (i.e., "King") constitutes an alert for the offense and they listen for the "live" audible that is going to be called next.

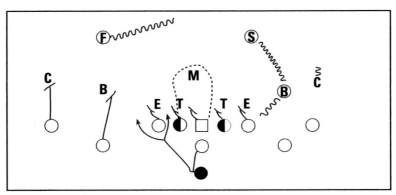

Diagram 2-1: Brown Honda Bo. The defense stems—"Oscar" is called to run toward the defensive weakness.

SPECIAL FEATURES

This system has some very unique special features. If a player forgets the snap count, instead of saying, "What's the snap count?" he can ask the player next to him what the count is by saying a predetermined term like "Cat" (or the team name). After hearing this code word, the player next to him should respond with a coded snap count term. Receivers should always watch the ball if they are confused about the snap count. Another term or hand signal can be used if the player forgets or does not hear the play selected. These terms and signals can be created for a system and are a very important part of this communication system.

This system also utilizes several No-Huddle tempos. Each tempo is used for specific reasons. Tempo use in the No-Huddle offense will be discussed in depth in Chapter Nine.

EVALUATION

This system might fit the needs of many programs because of the players' high retention of terminology. The terminology linking is very good; however, the terms could be remembered more easily if they were all categorized in subjects. If an athlete was not present when the original stories were told about the plays, then he would only remember the term as a word unto itself. If the terms are linked to something, such as the first letter of the term being described, and categorized in subjects for each facet of offensive football, the retention of terms and signals should be much higher. For example, if the runs were categorized by names of television show stars and passes were NFL teams, players would be able to discriminate between the two types of plays. However, the communication system can not become so simplified that the defense can begin to discriminate between terms during a game and know the play before it is executed. Terminology must be easy enough for the offense to understand and communicate, but complicated enough that the defense can not understand the language.

CHAPTER 3

NUMBER CODED SYSTEM

This system uses colors and numbers to communicate the entire offense to all offensive players. Every offensive player wears a wristband. These wristbands have four sections that represent different aspects of the offense. All sections have items numbered one through nine. The first three sections are color coded. The first section could be a pass or a run, the second section represents screens and specials, and the third column is also a pass or a run. The fourth section is colorless and identifies blocking schemes. A complete description of the numbering system and the function of the wristbands will be explained in the "signals" section.

PERSONNEL

The personnel are named similar to normal descriptive terms (X, Y, Z, T, F). The eligible runners and receivers are also given numbers to represent that position—for example, 7 (Z); 3 (tailback); 5 (fullback); and 1 (quarterback). These numbers are called as the last number in a progression of three numbers signaled and called in by the coach (i.e., Blue 273). If the play was a run, the three in this sample determines that the tailback will run the football.

FORMATIONS

Formations and the direction of the formation are signaled in by the coach. Terms are reduced to a combination of the term representing the formation and its direction. For example, a split right formation is called sprite and a split left formation is called splat. This approach reduces the number of terms and signals for formations by 50 percent (see Diagrams 3-1 and 3-2).

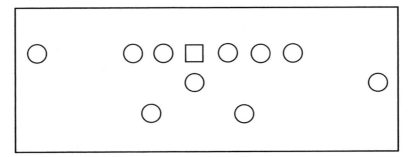

Diagram 3-1: Split right formation (sprite).

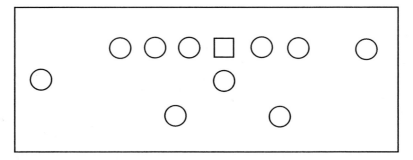

Diagram 3-2: Split left formation (splat).

MOTION

Many of the motions are built into the plays, with the motion man knowing the speed and direction of the motion according to the play that is selected. Other motions are called in a manner similar to other teams with terms like Zoom, Zip, Zap, Yank, Yo-yo, etc.

CADENCE

The snap count is tied into the color that is signaled in at the beginning of the play (see Figure 3-1). If gray is signaled from the sidelines, the play will be on two. If white is signaled, the snap count will be one. The placement of the colors on the wristband could change each week. The cadence always begins with the quarterback making the defensive front call and the pass protection call (i.e., Stack Lion). Stack tells the line that there is a 4-4 look by the defense and "Lion" tells the center to block toward the stack on the left if a pass is called. If a run is called, the front is still called and a dummy call can be made after the front call. For example, Stack Lion could be called again even though those terms are meaningless for the run called. Immediately following the front and protection call, the cadence begins with "set, hut, hut, hut," etc. The players are already set when the front is called by the quarterback.

SIGNALS AND DUMMY SIGNALS

The coach uses a body clock (Chapter Five) to signal in the play to the fullback, who makes the call to the rest of the offense. The quarterback is always under the center to keep the defense aligned and prepared for the play. A color is signaled in and followed by a series of three numbers. In special circumstances, an extra term might be signaled at the end of the three numbers to signify a play alteration.

Red (1) White (1)	Blue (2) Gray (2)	Brown (3) Black (3)	Blocking Schemes
1 Dash Pass	1 Middle Screen	1 Speed Option	1 Zone
2 Sweep	2 Throw Back Screen	2 Outside Zone	2 Play/Action Pass Pro
3 Counter Trey	3 Reverse	3 5-Step Pass	3 Crack
4 Toss	4 Screen Right	4 Blast (Iso)	4 G
5 Quick Trap	5 Draw Trap	5 Inside Zone	5 Base
6 Midline Option	6 Screen Left	6 Shuffle Pass	6 Trap
7 3-Step Pass	7 Hook 'n Lateral	7 Sprintout	7 Tag
8 Bootleg	8 Flea Flicker	8 7-Step Pass	8 Fold

( ) = snap count
Lightning = Red 947

Figure 3-1: Number code on player's wrist band worn by every player.

Every player on the team has a wristband and looks at the appropriate column for the color that is signaled (see Figure 3-1). The color determines which column to view on the wristband and it also identifies the snap count. The three numbers have specific meanings. The first number is the play number in that column. It could be a pass or run. If it is a pass, the next number is the protection and the third number is the pattern to be run. If it is a run, the second number would be the run blocking scheme and the third number the back running the football. No dummy signals are called from the sideline except when the number nine is signaled. Nine is a dummy number that tells each player to look at the next column and the next number in the call will be on the next column. However, at the line of scrimmage, the quarterback may use dummy signals often.

PASS PLAYS

A play may be signaled in as Black 386. Black tells the entire offense to look at the third column, which is color coded black. Three identifies the third play in that column, which is a 5-step drop pass. Eight identifies the pass protection to be used in this pass according to a pre-learned set of pass protection rules. Six is the pattern to be run by the receivers. Black determines the snap count of three. Pass patterns are taught instead of using a passing tree. All pass patterns and pass protection rules must be committed to memory and are not included in this discourse. See Figure 3-2 to view how each player would identify the play being run from the wristband.

PLAY/ACTION

The play is signaled in the same manner. If the call was White 325 (see Figure 3-3), the players look at the first column, because it is color coded white. Three identifies the third play in that column, which is a run. Since the play was a run, the second number is always found in the fourth column which identifies all run blocking combinations. Two identifies a term that represents play/action protection. Since the second number identified the play as a pass, the third number, five, determines the pass pattern to be run. In this offensive system, only one term represents the play/action pass, and it remains the same number in the same column every week for easier identification.

SCREENS/SPECIALS

Red 945 is the play signaled in. Red prompts the players to look at the first column. Since nine is a dummy number, the players look to the second column. Four tells the offense to run a screen to the right. The pass is thrown to the 5 receiver (see Figure 3-4).

Red (1) White (1)	Blue (2) Gray (2)	Brown (3) Black (3)	Blocking Schemes
1 Dash Pass	1 Middle Screen	1 Speed Option	1 Zone
2 Sweep	2 Throw Back Screen	2 Outside Zone	2 Play/Action Pass Pro
3 Counter Trey	3 Reverse	3 5-Step Pass	3 Crack
4 Toss	4 Screen Right	4 Blast (Iso)	4 G
5 Quick Trap	5 Draw Trap	5 Inside Zone	5 Base
6 Midline Option	6 Screen Left	6 Shuffle Pass	6 Trap
7 3-Step Pass	7 Hook 'n Lateral	7 Sprintout	7 Tag
8 Bootleg	8 Flea Flicker	8 7-Step Pass	8 Fold

( ) = snap count
Lightning = Red 947

Figure 3-2: Number code on player's wrist band worn by every player.

Red (1) White (1)		Blue (2) Gray (2)		Brown (3) Black (3)		Blocking Schemes	
1	Dash Pass	1	Middle Screen	1	Speed Option	1	Zone
2	Sweep	2	Throw Back Screen	2	Outside Zone	2	(Play/Action Pass Pro)
3	(Counter Trey)	3	Reverse	3	5-Step Pass	3	Crack
4	Toss	4	Screen Right	4	Blast (Iso)	4	G
5	Quick Trap	5	Draw Trap	5	Inside Zone	5	Base
6	Midline Option	6	Screen Left	6	Shuffle Pass	6	Trap
7	3-Step Pass	7	Hook 'n Lateral	7	Sprintout	7	Tag
8	Bootleg	8	Flea Flicker	8	7-Step Pass	8	Fold

( ) = snap count
Lightning = Red 947

Figure 3-3: Number code on player's wrist band worn by every player.

Red (1) White (1)	Blue (2) Gray (2)	Brown (3) Black (3)	Blocking Schemes
1 Dash Pass	1 Middle Screen	1 Speed Option	1 Zone
2 Sweep	2 Throw Back Screen	2 Outside Zone	2 Play/Action Pass Pro
3 Counter Trey	3 Reverse	3 5-Step Pass	3 Crack
4 Toss	4 Screen Right	4 Blast (Iso)	4 G
5 Quick Trap	(5 Draw Trap)	5 Inside Zone	5 Base
6 Midline Option	6 Screen Left	6 Shuffle Pass	6 Trap
7 3-Step Pass	7 Hook 'n Lateral	7 Sprintout	7 Tag
8 Bootleg	8 Flea Flicker	8 7-Step Pass	8 Fold

( ) = snap count
Lightning = Red 947

Figure 3-4: Number code on player's wrist band worn by every player.

PASS PROTECTION AND LINE CALLS

The pass protection scheme is always the second number of the call if a pass is signaled in. Play/action, sprint-out, quick pass, and drop-back protection schemes are all memorized by the offense. After a pass has been determined, the quarterback yells the front and determines the direction of the protection. If needed, the line will occasionally adjust the pass protection call of the quarterback. Line calls are made every down, with dummy calls a constant. The blocking schemes are built into the call for the run game, so very little scheme adjustment needs to be made.

OFFENSIVE HOLES

This system has no hole component. As in the memory link system, all plays are directional and conceptual; therefore, a numbered hole system is obsolete.

RUNNING GAME

Red 275 is the call signaled in by the coach. Red tells all offensive personnel to look at the first column for the play. Number two in that column is a sweep. The second number is the run blocking scheme and is found in the fourth column. The seventh item in that column is the type of run blocking scheme for the play. The ball will be given to the 5 player (see Figure 3-5). If the ball is always given to the same player on a particular play and/or if the blocking scheme is the same every time for a particular play, then the dummy numbers 99 can follow the color and the first number. For example, Red 299 means that the sweep is being run in the base blocking scheme with the 5 back running the ball, as he always does in this play.

AUDIBLES AND CHECK-WITH-ME'S

This system has no audibles or check-with-me's. This omission may be for philosophical or schematic reasons rather than communication purposes. If this system were adopted, a coach would have to invent the best possible method to implement audibles and check-with-me's in his own communication system.

OTHER SPECIAL FEATURES

This system has a Lightning feature in which the offense lines up immediately after a play is completed and runs a predetermined play on the first sound. This play is practiced all week and is run when the word Lightning is tagged on the previous play. For example, if the play is signaled Red 481 Lightning, the offense runs Red 481, and then runs Lightning on the very next play (see Figure 3-6). In this case the Lightning play is listed on the wristband as 947, which is a screen to the right to the 7 receiver. This play could be a big momentum shifter.

Red (1)⃝ White (1)	Blue (2) Gray (2)	Brown (3) Black (3)	Blocking Schemes
1 Dash Pass	1 Middle Screen	1 Speed Option	1 Zone
2 Sweep⃝	2 Throw Back Screen	2 Outside Zone	2 Play/Action Pass Pro
3 Counter Trey	3 Reverse	3 5-Step Pass	3 Crack
4 Toss	4 Screen Right	4 Blast (Iso)	4 G
5 Quick Trap	5 Draw Trap	5 Inside Zone	5 Base
6 Midline Option	6 Screen Left	6 Shuffle Pass	6 Trap
7 3-Step Pass	7 Hook 'n Lateral	7 Sprintout	7 Tag⃝
8 Bootleg	8 Flea Flicker	8 7-Step Pass	8 Fold

( ) = snap count
Lightning = Red 947

Figure 3-5: Number code on player's wrist band worn by every player.

Red (1) White (1)	Blue (2) Gray (2)	Brown (3) Black (3)	Blocking Schemes
1 Dash Pass	1 Middle Screen	1 Speed Option	1 Zone
2 Sweep	2 Throw Back Screen	2 Outside Zone	2 Play/Action Pass Pro
3 Counter Trey	3 Reverse	3 5-Step Pass	3 Crack
4 Toss	4 Screen Right	4 Blast (Iso)	4 G
5 Quick Trap	5 Draw Trap	5 Inside Zone	5 Base
6 Midline Option	6 Screen Left	6 Shuffle Pass	6 Trap
7 3-Step Pass	7 Hook 'n Lateral	7 Sprintout	7 Tag
8 Bootleg	8 Flea Flicker	8 7-Step Pass	8 Fold

( ) = snap count

Lightning = Red 947

Figure 3-6: Number code on player's wrist band worn by every player.

EVALUATION

This system is very effective and extremely difficult for the defense to decipher. The numbers on the wristband change each week, making it virtually impossible to break this communication system. The information is on the wristband for everybody, thus helping to eliminate mistakes due to memory lapses. One disadvantage is that this system is limited in the number of plays a team has available. For a coach who likes multiplicity in his offensive choices, this system might be too constricting. Additionally, it might be difficult to signal in any game adjustments to plays that are on the wristband if the defense is running schemes that are different from what was prepared for. Overall, this No-Huddle style of communication is successful and sound.

CHAPTER 4

THE GATHERING SYSTEM

This system has a "gathering" of the quarterback and the offensive linemen about two yards behind the football. The wide receivers are not involved in the "gathering." The four-wide receiver offensive scheme is the foundation for this No-Huddle style for several teams. After the play is signaled in, the play is called in the "gathering." The receivers know the play from the signal, but must listen very carefully to the call of the quarterback for any "hidden secret" or audibilized information. Each call by the quarterback at the line of scrimmage has a name or term, color, and number in it; some, none, or, all of the information from the quarterback is considered live. This system uses the "Hot" terms to represent live words or numbers and the "Cold" terms to represent dummy words or numbers. The gathering system uses a unique combination of colors, numbers and terms to communicate the offense. Even though the linemen gather behind the line of scrimmage, this style can be run at a quick tempo and be a very effective "hurry-up" style of offense.

PERSONNEL

All eligible receivers are identified by numbers. Receivers are numbered one to five, with one being the receiver on the left hand side and five being the receiver on the far right side (see Diagrams 4-1 and 4-2). Receiver numbers are used after a Hot name is called representing a pass, a primary receiver, and a particular route. For example, if "Bob" is the Hot term this week for a quick pass, the call at the line of scrimmage might be Bob Red 59 (see Diagram 4-3). This call tells everyone the play is a quick pass with the five receiver running a nine route and the other receivers running complementary routes.

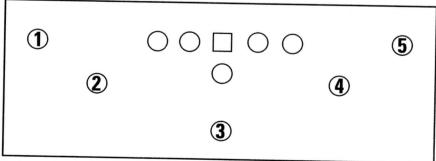

Diagram 4-1: Numbered receivers (deuce) formation.

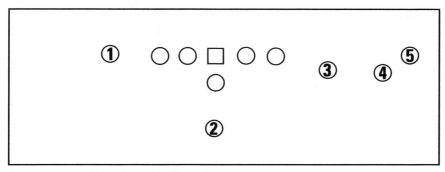

Diagram 4-2: Numbered receivers (trips) formation.

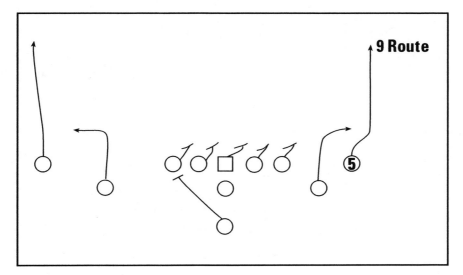

9 Route

Diagram 4-3: Bob Red 59.

Varied personnel groups can be used in this style; however, the four-wide receiver and single-back offensive scheme is utilized most often in this communication system. This structure could be adapted to any personnel substitution pattern desired.

FORMATIONS

Two schools of thought exist regarding how to handle formations. Some teams will allow the field position to dictate formation alignment at least 90 percent of the time. For example, if the ball is on the hash, then trips to the field is used. If the ball is in the middle, a doubles formation is used. In some cases, the play called will dictate the formation being used. Therefore, formations are rarely signaled and called, since the receivers choose the formation according to the field position. In the other method, the coach signals in a formation without direction and allows the receivers to align on their own. For example, if trips is signaled in and the ball is on the left hash, the receivers will most likely align in a trips right formation to the field. Both methods reduce the number of signals required and the amount of information that must be expressed and give the players more flexibility in formation alignments. In practice, many items are discussed regarding formation selection, receiver alignment, adjustments, and which plays will be run from what specific formations. If it is considered important for the coach to make formation decisions in the game, some signals and terms could be created to implement this aspect of the offense.

MOTION

Motion is rarely called in the gathering system. When motion is required, it is usually built into the play without any kind of signal or call. If the motion is not built in, the quarterback can nod to the receiver to get a boomerang motion for coverage identification (i.e., the receiver motions over and back to his original position to check for man coverage).

CADENCE

In this system, nearly every play is run on one. When teams start to really anticipate the count and come hard, the coach answers with traps, or, on some rare occasions, changes the snap count to two. Snapping the ball on one reduces offensive penalties and increases the chance of positive offensive play execution during practice and games. The cadence at the line of scrimmage is "set, hut, hut, hut," etc.

SIGNALS AND DUMMY SIGNALS

All signals are made from the sideline by three people wearing hats. One person is wearing a hat that is the Hot color. The coach dictates the play to be signaled in. All plays and formations are signaled according to their generic name (i.e., counter, draw, etc.). In the gathering and on the line of scrimmage, everything is translated to the coded language. Dummy (Cold) terms, colors and numbers are used constantly in this system so it is very difficult for the defense to identify the offensive information.

PASS PLAYS

All pass plays are on the players' wristbands (quarterback, running backs, and wide receivers) except the passes from the three-step passing game. Players learn a passing tree that is constructed for the receivers. For example, 359 Flood tells all the receivers what to do according to a passing tree. This play is coded "Noah" on the wristband and at the line of scrimmage. In the gathering, a color is called that determines whether the play is a pass with accompanying protection responsibilities, a run, a screen, or any other type of offensive play. For example, if Red is called in the huddle, the play is a run. If Black (sprint left) or Brown (sprint right) is called, the line knows that a pass has been called and what the protection is. If Blue is called, the play will be a 5- or 7-step drop-back pass with potential line pass protection adjustment calls made on the line of scrimmage according to the defensive front. Therefore, the call at the line might be Noah Blue 17. Noah is the pass pattern, Blue determines the protection, and 17 means absolutely nothing. The play is on one as usual.

The quick pass game is determined by Hot names at the beginning of the line call. For example, Red 16 is called in the gathering, which is a speed option to the right; however, the quarterback believes that he can hit the left outside receiver (1) with a deep fade route (9). He uses the Hot term "Bob" in his call at the line of scrimmage and says, "Bob Red 19." Bob alerts the offense that they will be executing a quick pass, probably to the one receiver on a nine route, with the other receivers running their corresponding complementary routes. Quick passes can also be called in the gathering by using "Purple" as the quick protection term. The receivers have already seen the signal (Purple) and know it is going to be a quick pass. The receiver and the number of the route will be called at the line of scrimmage based upon what the defense is showing the offense.

PLAY/ACTION

Pink is the color for play/action protection. The play is signaled in as Pink Counter Flood and this information is passed on to the linemen in the gathering. At the line of scrimmage, the quarterback yells, "Jack Pink 26." Jack is a Cold name, with Pink indicating the play/action and 26 explaining the fake run action by the backfield. The pattern is built into the play/action call. If a different pattern was desired, a term would be added telling the receivers to look at their wristbands for the pass pattern. The receivers really only need to look at their wristbands for pass patterns in this system, so it is imperative that coaches teach them to look at their wristbands on every play so they do not give away the pass and run game.

SCREENS/SPECIALS

Gray is the color that represents screen passes. The call from the coach might be Gray 58, which is a screen left. On the line of scrimmage, the call might be Sam Gray 58. Sam alerts the offense to the type of screen that will be thrown, with Gray telling the players a screen will be run and 58 identifying the action of the backfield prior to the throw. If this type of screen is run to the right and the left, then an "r" or "l" term could be used instead of Sam to determine direction (i.e., Ricky and Lucy).

COLORS	PASS PROTECTION
Black	Sprint Left
Brown	Sprint Right
Pink	Play/Action
Gray	Screen
Hot name or Purple	Quick Pass (3-Step)
Any other color	5-Step Passing Game

Table 4-1: Color chart for pass protection in the Passing Game The Gathering System.

PASS PROTECTION AND LINE CALLS

The pass protection is built in using colors. Once it has been determined in the gathering that a pass is being called and the pass protection color is given, the colors at the line of scrimmage can be dummy calls. All line and pass protection calls on the line of scrimmage are similar to those run at most schools. Table 4-1 shows the color chart for pass protection in the passing game. Since this style is run in the four-wide receiver offense, the number of fronts run by defenses is minimal and pass protection in the 5- and 7-step drop-back passing game is determined by the defensive front.

OFFENSIVE HOLES

The holes are numbered as in most other systems (see Diagram 4-4), with even numbers to the right and odd numbers to the left. These holes are very important to the success of the entire running game because the runs are called according to the holes.

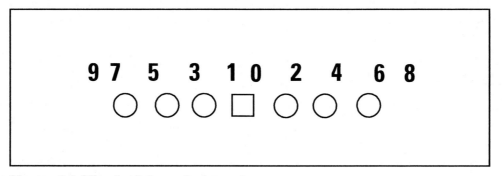

Diagram 4-4: Offensive hole numbering system.

RUNNING GAME

The running game is broken down into a series of numbers (i.e., 10's, 20's, 30's, 40's, 50's, 60's, etc. See Table 4-2). Each series refers to a type of run play that can be run at any hole called. For example, the 60 series refers to all direct runs. An inside zone run play to the right is called Red 62. The 50 series represents trap plays. An outside (long) trap to the left is called 55. These examples show the great flexibility of this system.

SERIES NUMBER	TYPE OF RUN
10's	Quarterback runs
20's	Options
30's	Counters
40's	Draws
50's	Traps
60's	Direct runs

Table 4-2: The Gathering running series

If Red is called in the gathering, the play will be a run unless it is changed at the line of scrimmage. Nearly every run is considered a check-with-me, and if the run is called in a certain direction in the gathering (i.e., Red 16), it will be run that way unless at the line of scrimmage the quarterback feels it should go the opposite way. If the play needs to go the opposite way, "Oscar" is called before the Cold color and the Cold number at the line of scrimmage. If the play call in the gathering was option check-with-me, then the team only needs to listen for an odd or even number to determine direction.

All run plays are signaled in by their normal names (i.e. speed option, counter trey, inside zone, etc.), but in the gathering the names are changed to numbers and at the line of scrimmage all runs are called according to their series number and the number of the hole being attacked. Some people might think that it is easy to identify a run by every Red call; however, once the run play has been called in the gathering, Cold colors, terms and numbers can be used at the line of scrimmage. For example, Red 55 was called in the gathering. If the quarterback called Purple 22 Noah at the line of scrimmage, it would mean absolutely nothing because they are all Cold colors, numbers, and terms. Therefore, 55 (trap left) is run. The use of Cold colors, terms, and numbers at the line of scrimmage helps maintain this secret communication system.

AUDIBLES AND CHECK-WITH-ME'S

This whole system is an audible. At the line of scrimmage, any run direction could be determined by either an "Oscar" call or an even or odd number with Cold colors and terms. The quick passing game can be audibilized using Hot terms. Any play can be changed to a completely different play by using the term "Charlie." Charlie tells the offense that the play has been changed and the call about to be made is actually the play that will be run. For example, if the play called in the gathering was Red 55 but at the line of scrimmage the quarterback noticed that the speed option right looked open, he would yell, "Charlie (changes the play) Red 28 (which is a speed option right)." In this offensive scheme, virtually every play is a check-with-me. The quarterback uses the built-in audible system to communicate the type and direction of the play to be run.

OTHER SPECIAL FEATURES

The signals used for the numbers are on a body clock, which will be discussed in Chapter Five. All other signals are creative ideas developed by the coaching staff and the players.

EVALUATION

This system is a very efficient communication system. It has enough flexibility to involve all aspects of offensive football. It allows the players to make decisions regarding formations, thus decreasing terminology and signal responsibilities. This system would take some time to learn, but once implemented it gives the coach a tremendous amount of flexibility in calling an offense. The only real negative item in this system is the lack of priority placed upon the cadence. The individuals running this system believe cadence is very overrated. If this system were adopted by a team for whom cadence variance was a high priority, the cadence could be developed further to vary the snap count as shown in Chapter 2 (page 20). This system has reduced the number of signals and terms needed by eliminating the formation and motion control by the coach. It is adaptable to any offensive scheme.

CHAPTER 5

DEVELOPING NO-HUDDLE COMMUNICATION

People in the world use many languages to communicate information to each other. In the same way, many different ways exist to communicate offensive information within a team. When implementing the No-Huddle style, many questions will invariably arise and must be addressed by the offensive staff in "brainstorming" sessions. This chapter will discuss not only brainstorming, but also idea formulation, communication suggestions and a unique system of No-Huddle communication.

Initially, many hours of brainstorming must be done with the offensive staff when trying to identify methods of communication, signals, and terminology as a foundation for an entire system of communication for the No-Huddle. These brainstorming sessions can turn out to be fun as well as productive. During the first meeting, several ground rules must be established regarding brainstorming sessions and idea formulation:

→ Plan 2-3 hours to meet in each brainstorming meeting.
  ⇒ The best ideas don't always come right away.

→ No idea is a bad idea.
  ⇒ Bad ideas may become stepping stones to great ideas.
  ⇒ All coaches need to feel ownership in this phase.

→ Set time limits for idea formulation and then evaluate ideas for the best ones.
  ⇒ After ideas are accepted, implement them.

→ Let everyone be involved.
  ⇒ Usually just coaches are involved.
  ⇒ Players can become involved in signals and some terms if allowed.
  ⇒ The system must be meaningful to coaches and players.

The brainstorming environment should be one free of judgment, with the sole purpose of developing the No-Huddle communication system without regard to whose ideas are best. Everyone involved should be contributing to this aspect of the offense. Once the system is in place, coaches can do revisions to it in a shorter amount of time. In 1995, after the first game at San Clemente, an athlete in the offense transferred to a rival school in the league. The offensive coaches met for two hours and developed an entirely new offensive communication system, complete with terms, numbers and signals. The players had the new system down after just two practices. The changes stayed within the original conceptual framework, which made the transition easier.

Players are very capable of adding to the communication system. When given the opportunity, players will come up with unique ideas for terms and signals in play development. The athletes take pride in ownership when they name a play or invent a signal, which improves retention of the information dramatically and also motivates players as they feel involved in the creative process.

Many questions need to be addressed when designing a No-Huddle communication system. When these questions are answered, the beginning of the system can be developed. The following two questions need to be addressed to begin stimulating thought for the type of No-Huddle system that will be employed:

→ Do you have an offensive system?

→ Is it organized and easy to communicate within a huddle?

If the current system used is organized and communicates efficiently within the huddle, a team should stay with that system of communication in the No-Huddle. Some modifications will be made to the terminology and signals to communicate this information outside the huddle, but if the system is organized, coaches should make an attempt to communicate the same ideas while staying within the same offensive schematic framework. If the method of communication that is currently employed is unorganized and confusing, the coaches should start from scratch in developing a system of communication. The following questions might help stimulate ideas for a new system of communication:

→ Do you use numbers or terms or both to communicate the offense?

→ Do you call passes using a numbered passing tree?

→ Do you have play series like 50's, 60's, 70's, 80's, 90's?

→ Do you name your receivers or give them numbers for identification?

→ How do you call your formations, motion, cadence?

→ Do you have line calls that are built into the play?

→ Do you number your holes and/or personnel?

→ How do you call your run game?

→ What about play/action, audibles, screens, specials, goal line package, etc.?

→ Is your communication simple and consistent?

Whatever the current system that is being utilized, a coach must decide how to communicate the necessary offensive information to the offense without the defense being able to understand the offensive communication system and gain an advantage. In the remainder of this chapter, a system of communication will be presented in all phases of the offensive scheme, with special attention given to a body clock, numbers and terminology, and signals.

Implementation of the No-Huddle system of communication can be difficult for the coach; however, if it is done effectively, the players will pick it up easily. If a coach told players that a draw play was called "Denver" and always referred to that play as "Denver," then the players would know that play only as "Denver." The coach will continue to refer to it as a draw play in his own mind, but the players are more apt to refer to it simply as "Denver." The same occurs for formations, personnel, motion or whatever else is communicated to the players. Coaches may have been taught a formation as spread formation, but if they name it "Wave," the players will only remember it as "Wave." Therefore, in order to run the No-Huddle, coaches must let go of their preconceived ideas and become open-minded in finding a way to implement the most effective communication system possible. The old adage "We've been doing it this way for as long as I can remember" may be reason enough to throw a term out and develop a new communication system. Coaches should not fall in love with an idea, especially if it is the only one they have. They should look for ways to be creative and develop a communication system that is meaningful to both the players and the coaches.

The following No-Huddle offensive system is organized, consistent and simple. The offensive scheme utilized will be the four-wide receiver, single-back offense. The run and pass plays shown will be basic ones, with the emphasis on how information is communicated, rather than how to execute the offensive play against various fronts and coverages. This style is a combination of numbers, terms, and colors and will be identified as the "Combination" system of No-Huddle. This system is an excellent one, but may not be the best for every team. Coaches should perform a careful analysis to determine which No-Huddle system will best fit an individual team's scheme and personality.

COMBINATION SYSTEM

Body Clock

In order to communicate numbers for any offensive system with numbers, a body clock must be developed. For years, baseball coaches have been using signals to communicate with players in strategic situations. Defensive football coaches have been using body clocks to communicate defensive information that is placed on a wristband. Since this method of number communication is sound, No-Huddle systems can utilize this proven technique to communicate numbers. Using a wristband has been a successful way to communicate an entire numerical offense (as shown in Chapter Three); however, in this discourse, the body clock is just part of a much larger communication system. Many ways may be used to communicate numbers on a body; however, when establishing a body clock system, the numbers should be on the body in a clockwise direction. The coach must determine where on his body the numbers are located. The following photos shows examples of numbers associated with the body clock. In this No-Huddle system, these numbers will be used for passing, running, motions and dummy calls.

BODY CLOCK

0—Top of the head　　　　　　　　　**1—Right ear**

2—Right shoulder

3—Right hip

4—Right knee

5—Left knee

6—Left hip

7—Left shoulder

8—Left ear

9—Chin

PERSONNEL (POSITIONS)

The personnel needs to be identified in order to tag receivers for route adjustments, determine who motions, and facilitate coaching adjustments. In this scheme, the personnel are given names because it is consistent with how the remainder of this No-Huddle scheme is communicated. The personnel will be named in certain parts of the run game, for motion responsibilities, when a route adjustment is called by the coach, or when a receiver is tagged by the coach for the quarterback to take a peek at hitting that particular receiver on a called route. In the four-wide receiver offense, all eligible personnel need to have a name (see Diagram 5-1). For the purpose of this illustration, the theme for naming the personnel will be famous comedy teams.

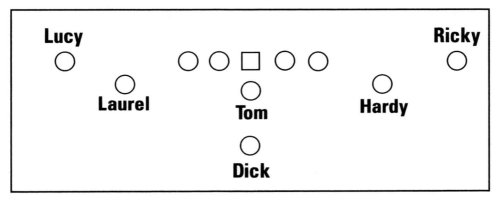

Diagram 5-1: Outside receivers never switch sides. Inside receivers can be moved by formation direction calls. (Try to keep to one or two syllables for personnel names.)

The signals for these terms can be very creative and fun, which leads to higher retention (see the following personnel signals). As discussed earlier, the athletes could come up with their own signals, thus lending ownership to the players. A coach must use discretion when using players' signals, recognizing the problems that can occur if an inappropriate signal is attempted.

Signal for "Laurel." Fingers move back and forth underneath the chin to simulate Stan Laurel fiddling with his bow tie.

Signal for "Hardy." Right hand up high to simulate Oliver Hardy taking his hat off to hit Stan Laurel with it. Drive right arm down and to the right to simulate Hardy hitting Laurel with his hat.

FORMATIONS

In this hypothetical offense, it is not critical to conceal formation communication from the defense. Therefore, communication of formations can be done in whatever terminology the coach determines. Listed below are some examples of different formations with their terms (Diagram 5-2 a-e). If it is important to conceal formations, numbers or terms could be used to identify formations.

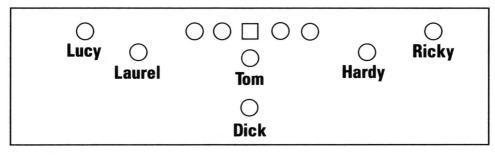

Diagram 5-2a: Right.

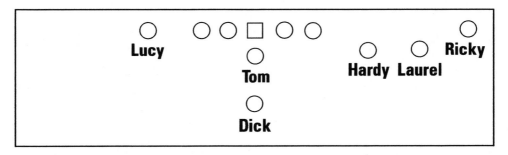

Diagram 5-2b: Spread right.

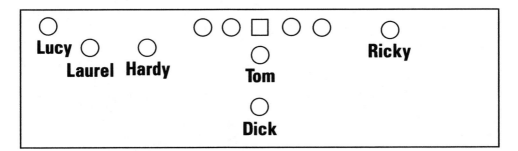

Diagram 5-2c: Spread left.

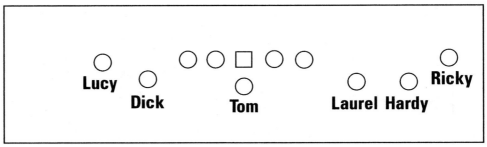

Diagram 5-2d: Ghost right.

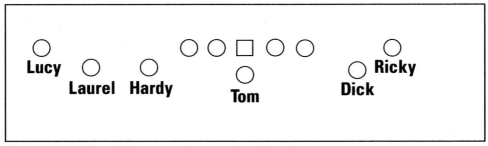

Diagram 5-2e: Ghost left.

Signals need to be used to communicate the play. Many teams will use two or three people to signal in a play (one as a live signal and the others as the dummy signals). The following signals are sample ideas for formations. Signals for right formations are done with two hands, while signals for left formations are done with one hand. The movements are the same for one-handed or two-handed motions.

Spread left—One hand is flat and in front of the body. Move the hand to the outside, simulating "spreading" butter on bread.

Spread right—Both hands are flat and in front of the body. Move both hands to the outside, simulating "spreading" butter on bread (looks like a "safe" call in baseball).

Receivers and backs are responsible for making alignment adjustments according to plays, instead of having a call for every possible alignment adjustment in each formation. These alignment adjustments in each formation are discussed thoroughly with the eligible personnel and practiced each day. This approach decreases considerably the amount of information that must be communicated between downs.

MOTION

Many teams must have a motion call in their play. However, some teams have motion built into their play selection. In this offensive scheme, both situations are employed. For the former, a play is signaled and called and the back or receiver who is supposed to motion knows when and how the motion is run according to the play selected. In this offensive scheme, the possibility exists that the type of motion and the motion man may need to be changed. Therefore, it is imperative that the motion be descriptive in terms and numbers. This offensive scheme has four types of motions that could be utilized (see Diagrams 5-3 a and b). The motions are given numbers to represent types of motion. Each position is given a name. After the formation call, the position term and a number will be called to determine who motions and how (Diagrams 5-4 a and b).

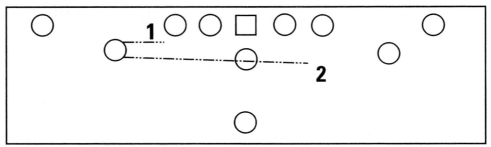

Diagram 5-3a: Two types of motion.

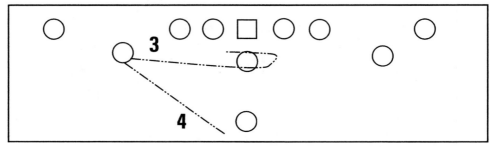

Diagram 5-3b: Two more types of motion.

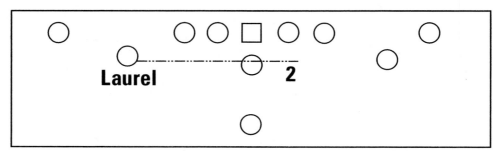

Diagram 5-4a: Laurel 2—The motion man and number (type of motion) must be called.

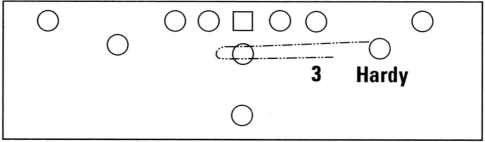

Diagram 5-4b: Hardy 3—The motion man and number (type of motion) must be called.

An example of a formation with a motion call is shown in Diagram 5-5.

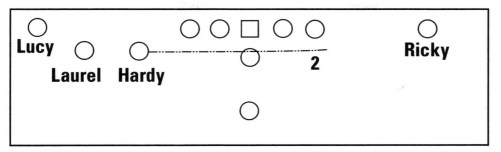

Diagram 5-5: Spread left Hardy 2.

The signal for this formation and motion is shown below.

Signal for Spread left—One hand in front and across the body.

Signal for Hardy—Right hand above head and down to simulate hitting Laurel on the head.

Hand on shoulder for number 2 on the body clock (refer to page 49).

CADENCE

Cadences vary from rhythmic to non-rhythmic and from lengthy to very brief. This system uses a cadence of "set, hut, hut," etc. The quarterback selects the cadence in most instances, except for specific tempos in the No-Huddle (see Chapter Nine). The reasons for changing the snap count are the same reasons used by a team that huddles up: to reduce the chance of the defense anticipating the snap count and getting an advantage on the line of scrimmage. The snap count does not always have to be communicated to the offense on every play. If a snap count is not given, the offense will go on the first "hut." Communication of the snap count is always done at the end of the play. A team must have a number of ways to call the snap count. Some examples of snap counts are listed below in Table 5-1 and other examples are found on page 20. These snap count ideas are based solely on progressive terms in order of occurrence. Signals for these terms are left up to the coach's own creativity.

FIRST SOUND	1	2	3
Peso	Penny	Nickel	Dime
Peso	Alpha	Beta	Omega
Peso	Baby	Boy	Man
Peso	Baby	Girl	Woman

Table 5-1: Snap count ideas (items that progress in order).

LIVE SIGNALS AND DUMMY SIGNALS

Many teams will signal a play in with two or three people. Only one person has the live signal; the others are dummy calls. In this system of communication, only the offensive coordinator signals in the play. He is completely responsible for the success or failure of the communication from the sideline to the offense. Quarterbacks can use nonverbal (hand) signals to indicate route adjustments for receivers and also send numerous dummy calls with those same nonverbal signals. If an efficient coded system is used, why would dummy signals and terms be needed? Dummy signals and terms must be used to prevent teams from deciphering signals or when teams begin to pick up on some signals, numbers, and/or terms. This system employs indicators (turn on and turn off) which tell the offense to not listen until the "turn on" indicator is said. For example, "Dark" means to turn off what is said until the word "Light" is heard, which tells the offense to listen to what comes next. A play may sound like this: Dark Denver Light Chicago Red Alpha. This call means that the play is a counter to the right on one (see Table 5-3, pg. 67). Coaches do not need to send in dummy signals on a consistent basis; however, the quarterback can make as many dummy calls as he feels comfortable with to throw off the defense. When scouting No-Huddle teams, some teams may try to film the signal and then the play to decipher the communication system, but if dummy signals are used effectively, the system will be too difficult to figure out. Teams who take this approach waste valuable time and effort in preparing to defend the communication system rather than the offensive scheme and personnel. In the past, teams have found that even using film to decode the communication system, they could not decipher the "coded" system. Dummy signals and terms are essential in this system to have an effective No-Huddle offense.

PASS PLAYS

The passing game can be a very complex part of an offense. This offensive scheme uses pass patterns rather than a passing tree. The pass plays are numbered in series, with route adjustments and the patterns labeled with terms. The pass protection schemes are built in with terms provided for line calls after the play has been called on the line of scrimmage. Many teams have a numbering system for their pass pattern series, usually 50's, 60's, 70's, 80's, and 90's. This offensive scheme will use the same numbering series and show how to communicate it within a No-Huddle framework.

In a normal huddle call, a pass play may be called Spread Right 56. This call gives the formation, the pass protection, and the pass pattern to be run. This play could be called in the same "string" in the No-Huddle offense and still be effective. If that is the only way the play is called, the defense will eventually figure out the call and the play. The best way to handle this problem is to come up with a variety of ways to call a 50 type of pass (3-step passing game). A great way to make this adjustment is to come up with a variety of things that are associated with the 50's. Some examples might be Grease, Chevy, Levi, and Twist. In addition to 56, a play could be called Levi 6, Grease 6, or Twist 6. The calls all have different signals except for the number signal, giving a coach using this system an endless number of possibilities to signal and call a play. In identifying terms, coaches should attempt to stay with one or two syllable words. This system can be applied to any series by identifying some things that occurred in each decade and inventing creative signals to communicate the information to the offense. If teams begin to pick up some of the signals or terms, identify another signal or term to use from that decade. The numbers are always signaled using a body clock. Table 5-2 shows some possibilities of examples for terms to be used in accordance with the passing series for each decade.

SERIES	NAMES			
50's (3-Step)	Grease	Levi	Chevy	Twist
60's (5-Step)	'Nam (Vietnam)	Nixon	Peace	Groovy
70's (7-Step)	Disco	Money	Bell (bottoms)	Tight (pants)
80's (Sprint Right)	Jackson (Michael)	Bush (George)	Vice (Miami)	Loose (clothes)
90's (Sprint Left)	Rap (music)	Sega (video games)	Clinton	Hammer (musician)

Table 5-2: Passing series names. These terms relate to each decade and are signaled in differently. Other terms for each decade could also be used.

Many times a coach may want to adjust a route in a given pattern or tag a receiver for the quarterback to take a peek at who is not part of his normal read progression. A route adjustment in a pattern can be accomplished by calling the play with a receiver term and a route adjustment term attached; for example, 63 Laurel Lotto (see Diagrams 5-6 a and b).

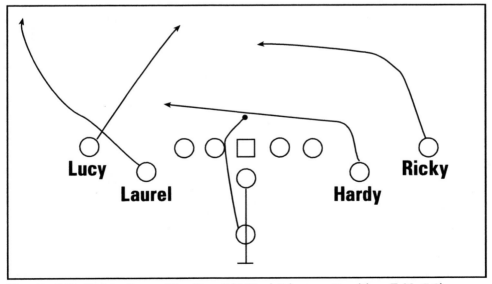

Diagram 5-6a: Pass pattern—63 or Nam 3 (5-Step); 3 (pass pattern) (see Table 5-2).

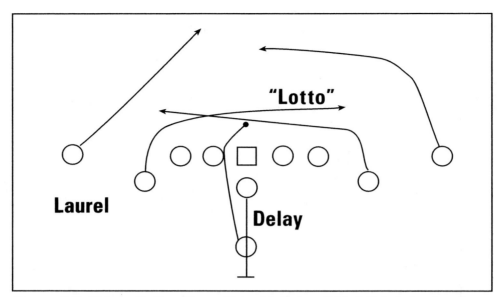

Diagram 5-6b: 63 Laurel Lotto or Peace 3 Laurel Lotto (see Table 5.2). Lotto is a term for a particular route adjustment.

To tag a receiver, the coach signals in the play with a "coded" receiver name attached to the end of the call; this tag alerts the quarterback to adjust his normal read progression and look at the tagged receiver first. For example, in the previous series, the backside corner really jumped the vertical route to his side, thus making the wheel route look open (see Diagram 5-6a for the pattern). Since that part of the pattern is not part of the normal quarterback read progression, the coach signals in 63 Laurel so the quarterback will look at Laurel first to see if he could complete a pass to him before going back to his normal read progression. Diagram 5-7 gives an example of a pass pattern with a formation and motion call. The formation call is Right, with Laurel 3 the reverse motion. Peace 4 is a 5-step pass with pattern number four. The term "Nickel" determines that the ball will be snapped on two. The play was signaled in to the quarterback using the terms demonstrated in the following photos.

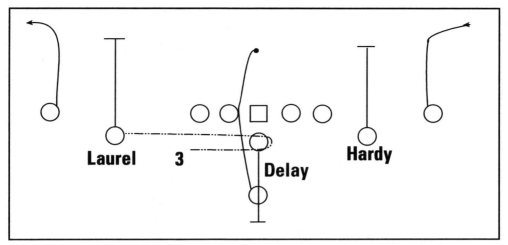

Diagram 5-7: Right (formation) Laurel 3 (motion); Peace (5-Step); 4 pattern; nickel snap count (Note—motion automatic for coverage identification).

Signal for right formation

Signal for Laurel

Number 3 on the body clock

Signal for peace

Number 4 on the body clock

Signal for nickel—hand showing five fingers—snap count is on two

PLAY/ACTION

Play/action passing is an extension of the passing game. If the quarterback ends up behind the center after a play/action fake, the protection scheme stays the same as in the 5- and 7-step drops, except with more aggressive blocking and less depth by the line. A term must signify that a play fake is being made. If the run is called "Denver," the play could be called Rambo Denver 3. Rambo means that it is a play action pass and Denver tells the backfield what the run action fake is. Three represents what type of pattern is being run in combination with the play/action (see Diagram 5-8). Therefore, whenever the offense hears "Rambo," they know the call is a play action pass. The backfield listens for the action and the quarterback and receivers listen for the pattern.

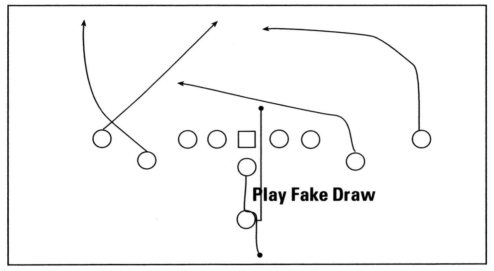

Diagram 5-8: Rambo (play/action)—Denver (run fake)—3 (pattern).

SCREENS/SPECIALS

Every team needs a couple of screens and specials that can be run at key times during a game. Since screens and specials are completely different categories of plays, they must be termed separately. In this system, screens will be categorized as fruits. The play is a middle screen to Ricky (see Diagram 5-9).

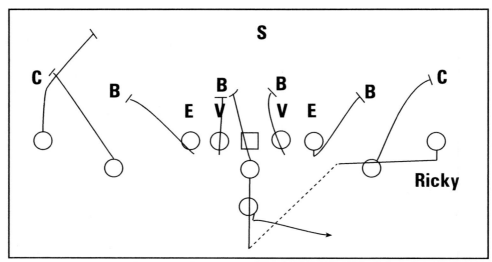

Diagram 5-9: Ricky Granny 7—middle screen to right outside receiver.

All middle screens are categorized as types of apples. This screen could be called Macintosh, Golden, Granny, or Red, along with the name of the receiver catching the screen. The play might be called Ricky Granny 7. Ricky tells who the pass is going to, Granny is the type of screen, and the seven makes the call sound like the rest of the play calls in the No-Huddle but has no meaning whatsoever. This same play could be called a number of different ways.

Specials could be American cars. Explorer 4 could be a hook and lateral. Explorer is the play, with four representing nothing, simply making the call sound like another play call. By placing these plays in different categories, the names could change each year or, if necessary, in the middle of the season or even each week.

PASS PROTECTION AND LINE CALLS

In the four-wide receiver offense, the defensive fronts that are seen are very limited. Therefore, the protection schemes can be very simple in the 5- and 7-step passing games. Depending upon the dynamics of the front and potential blitzing linebackers, the center will make his call for protection. The protection schemes are based entirely upon the defensive front. These schemes are practiced each day in blitz pick up periods, so very little communication is needed for line calls on game night. If a team puts seven men in the box (man blitz), a special man blitz package is executed. On 50 passes the line will turn either left or right, depending upon which direction the quarterback intends to throw to. If a line call needs to be communicated, the call will be made immediately following the play call. The quarterback will hesitate a count before starting the cadence to ensure that all line communication has been completed.

OFFENSIVE HOLES

In this system of communication, players are not required to learn holes. Offensive players must understand the concept of the play and the general area that is being attacked. Linemen learn the technical aspect of each play and are prepared for any adjustable contingencies based on defensive fronts and basic defensive alignments.

RUN GAME

The run game can be communicated in a variety of ways. In this offensive scheme, the runs are given terms. All runs are names of professional football teams, their cities, and a great player from that team. Three different terms represent the same play. The city's first letter is identical to the run play's first letter. For a listing of run plays, see Table 5-3 below.

TYPE OF RUN	CITY	TEAM NAME	PLAYER
Draw	Denver	Bronco	Elway
Inside Zone	Indy	Colts	Marshall
Outside Zone	Oakland	Raider	Howie
Trap	Tampa	Bucs	Dilfer
Speed Option	Seattle	Hawks	Blades
Counter	Chicago	Bears	Payton

Table 5-3: Run game terminology—professional football theme.

After the run term, the quarterback adds a direction term (color) that tells the offense which direction the play is being run. Terms that have an "r" in them tell the team the play is being run to the right and terms with a "l" in them determine a run play to the left. The terms and signals are limitless. For example, a play might signaled in Denver Orange 5. Denver means draw play, with Orange meaning to run the play to the right and 5 meaning nothing. Listed in Table 5-4 are three different terms called for the run game that mean exactly the same thing. The number at the end of a run call means absolutely nothing; it is simply added to make all types of plays sound alike.

THREE DIFFERENT WAYS TO CALL THE SAME PLAY
Denver Orange 8
Bronco Red 3
Elway Brown 6

Table 5-4: Draw play to the right.

Diagram 5-10 shows a complete play with a formation and motion call. If the snap count is not signaled in, the quarterback has the option of the count, but usually snaps the ball on one. On certain plays like this one, motion is built into the play and does not need to be signaled. The signals used to signal in the play are shown in the following photos.

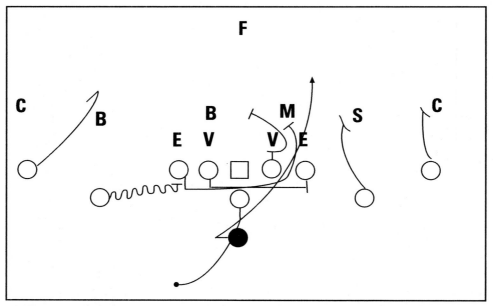

Diagram 5-10: Right (formation) Laurel 1 (motion)—Bears (counter)—Brown 6 (right).

AUDIBLES AND CHECK-WITH-ME'S

Audibles are typically unnecessary in the No-Huddle style because the entire offense is essentially an audible system. At times in extreme cases, a blitz adjustment must and can be made in a pre-snap look. During these unique circumstances, the quarterback will yell "Easy" in a long, drawn out, monotone voice to change the play call and implement the blitz package adjustment for that week.

Signal for right formation—motion is built into the play

Signal for Bears (counter)—claws

Signal for Brown (run play to the right)—Dirt

Number 6 on the body clock—the number means nothing in this call

Check-with-me's are very common plays that are run at all levels of football. Whether the quarterback is looking for a "3" technique or an extra linebacker or coverage shells, one play is usually called based upon the defensive indicator. The check-with-me system is easily employed within this communication system. The quarterback is signaled the play with a descriptive check after the play, or if the game plan dictates, every time the play is called it is a check-with-me. Based upon the defensive indicator, the quarterback yells the correct play to the offense and runs the play. If the defense stems after the play is selected and the play needs to be run the opposite direction, the Oscar call can be made. Check-with-me's are very effective when defenses align quickly. If defenses start to disguise or stem often, the coach can utilize the Up tempo to get the defense aligned more quickly and give the quarterback a better look with check-with-me's (this concept of Up tempo will be discussed more in depth in Chapter Nine). The tempos of the No-Huddle style give the coach a weapon to improve the opportunity for a check-with-me system of plays.

OTHER SPECIAL FEATURES

This system employs the use of multiple tempos, which will be discussed in Chapter Nine. These tempos add another dimension to the explosiveness of the No-Huddle offense. The mechanics of this style will be explained more in depth in Part II of this book.

EVALUATION

In this chapter, a No-Huddle communication system was developed. The methods for formulating ideas through brainstorming sessions and maintaining group integrity when developing new ideas were explained. This communication system was developed and delineated through various aspects of the offensive structure. The combination system is an excellent system that is easily adaptable to any offensive scheme.

In Part I, several systems of communication were discussed. This chapter was designed to give the reader a clear understanding of some ways to communicate a No-Huddle offense. It should be a springboard for ideas to develop a style that is conducive to any offensive system. In Part II, the mechanics of the No-Huddle offense will be explored, with the emphasis placed upon the combination No-Huddle style.

PART 2

COMMUNICATION MECHANICS

Communication mechanics are the methods used to install and execute the No-Huddle style in any offense. In the previous chapters, special attention was paid to the different systems that are currently being used in successful offenses, with the final chapter exploring No-Huddle communication development. Once the communication system is in place, a coach must know how to execute this style of offense within any offensive structure. The chapters in this section will discuss how to teach, practice, and execute the No-Huddle offense. The offensive scheme used with this style in the ensuing chapters will be the four-wide receiver offense.

The combination style of No-Huddle will be discussed with special emphasis on the tempo's impact on offensive success. The first chapter in this section explores the best methods used to teach the No-Huddle style and produce excellent results. In the practice chapter, an entire week of practice is discussed with special notes on how to adapt the No-Huddle style to any practice structure. In the eighth chapter, a game plan is developed with an emphasis placed upon attacking defenses with the No-Huddle style. Game management is introduced and how to run the No-Huddle style in game situations is presented. Chapter Nine discusses the heart of the No-Huddle: controlling the tempo of the game. The coach can really help control the rhythm of the game and gain a tremendous advantage over the defense by adjusting the tempo.

The last chapter is a summary of the main points with a major emphasis on taking a risk to improve the offensive production of any offense. Success as a high school coach depends largely on always being aware of their personnel strengths and weaknesses. This awareness can have an effect on the type of offensive scheme that is employed in order to be successful. Whatever the scheme employed, the No-Huddle style can be used to help add another dimension to the scheme to enhance offensive success.

CHAPTER 6

TEACHING THE NO-HUDDLE

Teaching the No-Huddle offense can be fun and easy. When teaching any communication system, whether it is in the huddle or not, time must be invested in teaching nomenclature that can be used to communicate the information to the offense from the coach. As shown in Chapters Two through Five, many methods exist for communicating information; however, for the remainder of this book, emphasis will be placed upon the method described in depth in Chapter Five. In this chapter, the combination No-Huddle system will be used in describing how to teach the communication system, in what order to teach it, and what methods to use when teaching. Additionally, brief discussions will be presented with regard to two-way players, conditioning, and key coaching points in this style.

High school football coaches usually have more time to coach than coaches at any other level of football. Before two-a-days begin in August, high school coaches can utilize spring football and most of the summer for "football camps." This time usually allows a coach to interact with players approximately thirty days more than college coaches are allowed. Time should not be a factor for an organized coach to teach the No-Huddle. If implemented in spring football, the No-Huddle system of communication should be in full swing by the end of spring practice.

Many coaches will argue that players in college and the NFL can handle the extra mental load associated with the No-Huddle, but that it is too difficult for the high school football player. This belief is a misconception, as players at the high school level have demonstrated the ability to not only learn but also excel in the No-Huddle system. Many of our players are in special resource programs at school and adapt to this style quite easily. If the No-Huddle is taught correctly, it is just as easy, or even easier, to learn than any other type of huddled communication system. Players assimilate the "coded" system and really enjoy and are motivated by this "secret language" they come to know.

Players can and should be involved in the development of the No-Huddle communication system. Coaches usually do not allow the athletes to be involved in the development of offensive schemes, but they can be involved in developing creative ideas of communication. Coaches need to communicate this information to the players, so the players can understand the system and identify with it. The

Signal for Bugs Bunny (blast)—ears

Signal for Daffy Duck (draw)—hand open representing a duck's beak—hand closing like a duck's beak shutting to simulate a quack

coaches can set the descriptive parameters for the players and then let them have fun coming up with play terminology and signals. For example, all runs are named after cartoon characters, so the players come up with the characters and the signals; "Bugs" Bunny might represent a blast, "Daffy" Duck might be a draw, etc.

The coach can veto anything he does not like, but he must try to stimulate thought by the players in the early development of this system. The environment for creating terminology should be positive and open to any and all ideas. Coaches should make every attempt to encourage athlete participation and try to include at least one idea from everybody to establish team and individual ownership. Once the system is in place, some minor communication adjustments might be needed in the future, and athlete involvement may become purely optional. After the No-Huddle offensive system has been run for at least a year and the system has proven to be successful, the coach does not need to develop a new system the next year. This old communication system will be taught to the next group of players with very little input from them, but with the idea that former players helped develop the system. Some subtle communication and scheme adjustments can be made in the future.

HOW TO TEACH THE NO-HUDDLE

If this system is run at the high school level, the terminology and communication system should be taught at the freshman level for easy transition between levels all the way to the Varsity. Special attention should be paid to make sure that the lower level programs are not actually running the No-Huddle offense, but just using the terminology. The potential for opponents to decipher the system is much higher at a lower level football game with very little crowd noise. Coaches might not want to have the lower levels communicate this way if there is a high turnover rate of coaches and/or players in the program.

An initial "brainstorming" meeting should be called where the only writing done is by the coach on the whiteboard. The players are just throwing out the ideas. As discussed in earlier chapters, any idea is a good one at this point. Once the system has been developed, the process of teaching the No-Huddle begins.

If this process took place one year earlier, the old No-Huddle terminology and numbering system must be taught. To teach the old communication system, the No-Huddle meetings should last no more than thirty minutes. If they are presented with too much information initially, the players might become confused and unmotivated. Therefore, the coach should teach the system in small portions and review often early in the process.

ORDER TO TEACH THE NO-HUDDLE

Initially, the entire concept of communication should be taught. All terms and numbers should be taught concurrently with signals. Then the parts of the No-Huddle system should be taught in the following order:

→ Body clock
→ Personnel (positions)
→ Formations
→ Motions
→ Cadence
→ Passing game
→ Route adjustments
→ Running game
→ Pass protection and line calls
→ Play/action passing
→ Dummy signal system
→ Audibles and check-with-me's
→ Other special features (i.e. alerts, "easy," tempos, etc.).

TEACHING METHODS USED

The coach should lecture, demonstrate, and randomly ask the players questions when disseminating the information involved in the No-Huddle. The best method of teaching is whole-part-whole. In this method the "whole" concept is presented first, which may be overwhelming for the athletes. Next the information is broken down into "parts," or pieces of information, for better understanding and higher retention. Once all of the parts have been taught, then the "whole" concept is presented again for optimal learning.

In the beginning, the entire communication system and concepts are explained briefly. The players may feel mentally taxed at this point. Then the coach breaks the system down into small parts and teaches each part separately. For example, the coach may demonstrate the body clock and have the players draw a body on their sheet of paper and attach the numbers accordingly. The coach may then teach the formations and motions with terms, signals and diagrams. Players write down diagrams, terms, and signals on their paper. After each part has been taught, then the coach teaches the "whole" concept again for higher retention. During the early part of learning the system, the coach should question players randomly and often.

Reciprocal teaching is then employed by the players between teaching sessions. They should quiz each other on the terminology and the signals whenever and wherever they can. After approximately three sessions, a written test is given to the players regarding the aspects of the communication system taught to that point (see Figure 6-1). This first exam tests for terminology, numbers, and signal recognition. In future tests, the schematic and technical concepts of the offense will be emphasized in combination with the No-Huddle system of communication. The exam in Figure 6-1 evaluates whether the athletes know the signals for each term, color, and number. The athletes write the correct item in the space provided after the signal has been given by the coach. To save time, the coach can videotape this "signal" test and then play the videotaped test each year. He should also make a correction key for the exam and keep it in a safe place.

NO HUDDLE TEST #1

In this test, you will be required to recognize signals and place the terms, numbers, and colors corresponding with those signals in the spaces provided below. Make sure that your writing is legible so the coach can correct your answers. Put the correct answer for the signals in the spaces provided:

Formations	Numbers	Terms and/or Colors
1.	10.	20.
2.	11.	21.
3.	12.	22.
4.	13.	23.
Motions	14.	24.
5.	15.	25.
6.	16.	26.
7.	17.	27.
8.	18.	28.
9.	19.	29.
		30.

Regular testing makes the players accountable for learning the information. At San Clemente High School, in addition to No-Huddle tests, we give written tests each week on game day to determine whether the players know their responsibilities, know their opponent, etc. Each position coach writes a test for each of his players based on what he expects them to know for the game. The coach corrects the exam and reviews the test with his players in the pre-game meeting to ensure optimum mental preparation.

Players need to know the communication system of the No-Huddle offense. Initially, coaches should make it known to the players that if they do not know the play, they can not compete for the position. This expectation is usually motivation enough for the athletes to learn the system. The previously explained teaching methods are used to increase retention at a faster rate, therefore allowing more attention to be placed upon scheme and technical teaching to improve offensive performance. During practices, an assistant coach will randomly question players standing behind the offensive drill or on the sideline regarding what the play is going to be and what the signal was. This strategy makes the players pay constant attention to the coach signaling in the play during every practice period, thus improving retention and decreasing "horseplay."

The terminology for the combination communication system should be structured according to categories. The first letter of the play being taught should be the same as that of the "coded" term used to identify it. For example, earlier in the chapter, "Bugs" or "Bunny" was used to describe a blast run play and "Daffy" or "Duck" was used to describe a draw play. These terms begin with the first letter of the name of the play being described. The category of terms being used (cartoon characters) also relates well to high school athletes. Careful planning and selection of categories for terms can have a dramatic impact on the retention of information by high school students. The coach should make the communication system fun, flexible, and relative to the players.

TWO-WAY PLAYERS

The high school football coach must have a philosophical stance on whether to use a two-platoon or one-platoon system. Because the game is approximately 33 percent longer in the No-Huddle, careful attention must be directed to determining whether the team will be two-platoon or one-platoon. The philosophy at San Clemente High School has always been to try to use a two-platoon system; however, in six years there has never been a true two-platoon team. The following philosophical tenets are the foundation of the San Clemente football program:

→ A team wins with its best athletes on the field.

→ Defense wins championships.

- → Offense gets first pick for a quarterback, running back, wide receiver, and center.
- → Defense gets first picks on all of the rest of the athletes.
- → Two-way players are usually seniors and good athletes who started on one side of the ball as juniors (usually defense).
- → During spring football, the two-way player practices on his "new" side of the ball exclusively.
- → When fall begins, practice is organized to share the two-way athletes or have offensive and defensive emphasis type of practices.
- → A player is labeled mainly a "defensive" or an "offensive" player, thus determining when he gets rest during the game.
- → Prior to the game, coaches discuss when and on what side of the ball the two-way players will be rested.

Each year approximately two to four players play both ways for San Clemente. These players are usually physically gifted athletes with varied levels of intelligence. They must have a strong work ethic and a desire to play both ways. Even though they are extremely well conditioned, they will still need some rest during the course of the game. These two-way players usually play full-time on one side of the ball and approximately 3/4 of the time on the other side of the ball. Some of the most highly conditioned athletes have never come off of the field. Coaches must be keenly aware of the fatigue factor when selecting and playing two-way players.

The No-Huddle still gives the offense the advantage because the opponents' two-way players get very tired and will not be able to perform at the same level or for the same amount of time as they are accustomed to. For example, two years ago a team we played continued to have "equipment problems" with the hope of delaying the game and giving their players a chance to catch their collective breaths in the fourth quarter. The officials finally sent the athlete off of the field and required a substitution. In many instances, defensive linemen won't even get in a stance in the third and fourth quarters because of fatigue. The increased number of plays really hurts teams that have numerous two-way players.

CONDITIONING

Conditioning is a large part of the No-Huddle system. Since the entire team must be prepared to play a game that is one-third longer than normal, conditioning must be an integral part of the No-Huddle system. Creating a practice environment that produces an attitude emphasizing conditioning as a way to gain an advantage over other teams increases the motivation of the athletes to perform well in these periods. Conditioning is stressed starting in the spring and continues throughout the entire summer. Conditioning is the physical foundation of a good No-Huddle team.

Key Coaching Points

→ Linemen should have their elbows on their thighs in a "ready" position waiting for the call.

→ Hustle should be stressed at all times and in all practice periods.

→ The coach will always signal in plays from the side and then coach from behind the offense during practice.

→ Once concepts are learned, tempos can be practiced (see Chapter Nine).

When teaching concepts, an exam is usually given to the students to evaluate how well the information was learned. Quizzes are usually given to test the "parts" leading up to the big exam. Once the exam is given, the teacher, the student and hopefully the parents know the results of the exam. The teacher in the classroom is not usually evaluated on the performance of his or her students, but the coach on the football field is evaluated very closely every week. In high school football, the final exam is taken every Friday night in front of thousands of people. Therefore, the teacher (coach) and the student (player) must make every effort to be physically, mentally, and emotionally prepared for each final exam every Friday night.

CHAPTER 7

PRACTICING THE NO-HUDDLE

The purpose of practice is to prepare an offense to be successful each week against all opponents. The main objectives of a practice are scheme development and the improvement of players' condition and technique. Many components in practice organization vary from team to team in regard to offensive scheme, philosophy, and personnel. In this chapter, practice organization will be presented as it relates to a No-Huddle four-wide receiver offense. The No-Huddle practice is very similar to a traditional practice. The main objectives are the same as above but are coupled with an increased opportunity for improved play execution through additional repetitions of the offensive plays within the scheme. The increased repetition of practice plays (repetitions double) occurs in each period because of the No-Huddle speed. The execution also improves because the defense will run base fronts and coverages which allow the offense to practice a multitude of plays against limited defensive looks. These practices are designed to be implemented with a 50-player roster; however, practice could be adapted to meet the needs of the team implementing the No-Huddle. This practice structure could vary with a one-platoon team.

This chapter will also discuss a "normal" high school game week of practice preparation in the No-Huddle four-wide receiver offense. Each practice period may be similar to that of a huddled team, but special emphasis will be placed upon the unique No-Huddle circumstances. In a No-Huddle practice, different tempos must be utilized and unique nuances must be identified and executed. The No-Huddle coach must be very flexible, because true "scripting" of plays can have an adverse effect on offensive tempo. Scout team management, use of two-way players in practice, key coaching points in No-Huddle practices, and No-Huddle opponents' practice sessions will also be addressed.

Each week of practice begins with the basic game plan to be implemented (see Chapter Eight). The daily offensive installation will be written on the back of each practice sheet in a specific format according to the offensive period being run. These items will form a key part of a No-Huddle practice session. The coach will write a "play checklist" on the back of each practice schedule for easy access and to ensure that the game plan gets practiced during the week in an effective manner. Most teams will script plays in an offensive practice; however, in the No-Huddle, scripting can inhibit tempo variations and decrease repetitions

```
RUN                 FRONTS
Inside Zone         4-3 (2x)
Outside Zone        4-4 (2x)
Speed Option
Draw
QB Sneak (Alert)
```

Figure 7-1: Play checklist for run period on a Monday.

in practice. The "play checklist" (see Figure 7-1) is the No-Huddle style equivalent to scripting in "huddled" offenses. The plays can still be managed and practiced effectively without formal scripting. This checklist is prepared for each period that requires specific plays to be practiced against specific fronts in specific situations.

PLAY CHECKLISTS

Coaches must use memory and flexibility when running the No-Huddle style. Many coaches will script their practices for specific plays to be run against specific defenses in certain situations. This type of game planning is focused upon the situation. The No-Huddle offense is predicated upon the defensive scheme executed, and not just the down and distance or field position. Coaches will call plays according to the defenses shown in the game; therefore this type of reactionary play selection must be practiced by the coach during the week (see Chapter Nine for information on tempos and how to make the defense declare their front and coverage). In practice, the coach will call a play based upon the defense seen. The defensive scout coaches are given a sheet of the fronts and coverages and told how many times to run each particular defense during each period of practice. This approach improves the coach's ability to memorize the game plan, recognize defenses to call the play, and react to the defensive scheme during the rhythm of the game.

The structured coach likes the scripted format where each situation is practiced. How many times in a game are plays called according to a script? Very few. Therefore, the coach should become accustomed to developing a rhythm of play selection in practice according to the defensive scheme, and previous play success. The flexibility in this structure can be intimidating to a highly structured person. At BYU everything was scripted, and I became very used to this structure. It was difficult to make the transition to this type of play selection and practice structure, but well worth the effort.

Each "play checklist" is written on the back of the practice schedule and prepared prior to each practice. The coach knows what plays are on the checklist and starts to call the plays according to the defense in each skelly and team period. After each play is called, an assistant checks that play off the list. Some plays that are not on the checklist may be called in the period according to the defensive scheme presented. This flexibility must be attained to simulate a typical game situation in calling plays. Toward the end of each practice period, the assistant coach overseeing the checklist will tell the offensive coordinator what plays, if any, on the list have not been called. The coach will then make sure that the remaining plays are practiced in that period to ensure optimum game preparation through practice. The concept of the "Play Checklist" helps improve the coach's retention of the game plan for the week and his ability to react to game situations and rhythms with greater ease.

PRACTICE SCHEDULES

Monday is the first practice of the week. The players have not yet viewed the opponent on film. The team will meet for a brief time on Monday during the football class to discuss the upcoming opponent's personnel and defensive scheme. The players will then come to practice at 2:50 p.m. (see Figure 7-2 a-d for typical weekly practice schedules). The coaching staff (eight coaches) coach on only one side of the ball. The left side of each practice schedule represents offensive coaches' responsibilities in practice. Items on the right side are the defensive coaches' responsibilities. The practice schedule is designed according to times rather than just "practice periods." Each coach is given a practice schedule to ensure efficient time management during practice.

Practice times and lengths vary from day to day, but the weekly schedule remains consistent throughout the season. The "play checklist" for each period and goals for the day (see Figure 7-3 for a sample Tuesday "play checklist") are written on the back of each practice schedule for the offense. Space is provided for the coach to write notes for any adjustments or comments about the practice. In the following pages, a complete description of each practice period will be explored.

MEETINGS

Since time is extremely limited in public high school, players are asked to watch film just twice a week for approximately 45 minutes during lunch. During these film sessions, the players view the upcoming opponents on Monday, and on Thursday watch the previous night's team and goal line practice periods. If players have free time, film is made available to them throughout the day. At this point, the No-Huddle communication system has been installed successfully and is well established, and more attention is paid to the offensive scheme.

TRITON FOOTBALL PRACTICE SCHEDULE

Pre Practice: Meetings/Walk-Thru 5th per.   Date: Mondays
Dress: Full Pads   Field: Main

T	QB'S	RB'S	WR'S	O LINE	D LINE	I LB	OLB	DB'S
2:50	Stretch							
3:05	Offensive Impl.	O Impl.	O Impl.	O Impl.	Set Recognition	Set Rec.	Set Rec.	Set Rec.
3:40	Indiv.	Indiv.	Indiv.	Indiv.	Indiv.	Indiv.	Indiv.	Indiv.
3:45	Blitz Walk-Thru	Blitz Walk-Thru	1-on-1	Blitz Walk-Thru	Stunts	Stunts	Stunts	1-on-1
3:55 Skelly	O Skelly	O Skelly	O Skelly	7-on-7 Run	7-on-7 Run	7-on-7 Run	7-on-7 Run	0
4:15	Water							
4:20	O Run	D Skelly	O Run	O Run	O Run	D Skelly	D Skelly	D Skelly
4:40	Team O							
4:55	Condition							
5:10	Lift							

Blocking and tackling with the head making the initial contact is illegal—don't do it!

Figure 7-2a: Sample Monday practice schedule given to each coach and posted for player viewing.

TRITON FOOTBALL PRACTICE SCHEDULE

Pre Practice: Early Outs 1:05 P.M.
Dress: Full Pads

Date: Tuesday
Field: Main

T	QB'S	RB'S	WR'S	O LINE	D LINE	I LB	OLB	DB'S
1:20	Stretch							
1:35	PAT/PAT Block K.O.R. KO Cover Punt Block	Legsavers Legsavers						
2:00	O Team Blitz	O Team Blitz	O Team Blitz	O Team Blitz	O Team Blitz	O Team Blitz	O Team Blitz	O Team Blitz
2:15	Condition Screen Specials	Condition Screen Specials	Condition Screen Specials	Condition Screen Specials	Condition Pursuit	Condition Pursuit	Condition Pursuit	Condition Pursuit
2:30	Water							
2:35	GL (D)	GL (D)	GL (D)	GL (D)	GL (D)	GL (D)	GL (D)	GL (D)
2:45	GL (O)	GL (O)	GL (O)	GL (O)	GL (O)	GL (O)	GL (O)	GL (O)
2:55	Indiv	Indiv	Indiv	Indiv	Indiv	Indiv	Indiv	Indiv
3:10	1-on-1 GL	1-on-1 GL	1-on-1 GL		Stunts	Stunts	Stunts	1-on-1 GL
3:20	O Run	D Skelly	O Run	O Run	O Run	D Skelly	D Skelly	D Skelly
3:35	Team D	Team D	Team D	Team D	Team D	Team D	Team D	Team D
4:05	Team O	Team O	Team O	Team O	Team O	Team O	Team O	Team O
4:30	Done							

Blocking and tackling with the head making the initial contact is illegal—don't do it!

Figure 7-2b: Sample Tuesday practice schedule.

TRITON FOOTBALL PRACTICE SCHEDULE

Pre Practice: Lift 4:30; Early Outs 5:15

Dress: Full Pads

Date: Wednesday

Field: Main

T	QB'S	RB'S	WR'S	O LINE	D LINE	I LB	OLB	DB'S
5:30	Stretch							
5:45	Punt Cover / Punt Ret. / Punt Blk.	Legsavers						
6:05	Indiv	Indiv	Indiv	Indiv	Indiv	Indiv	Indiv	Indiv
6:15	Green Skelly	Green Skelly	Green Skelly	Live Stunts	Live Stunts	Live Stunts	Live Stunts	Green Skelly
6:25	Blitz PU	Blitz PU	D Skelly	Blitz PU	Blitz PU	D Skelly	D Skelly	D Skelly
6:40	Team O	Team O	Team O	Team O	Team O	Team O	Team O	Team O
6:55	Water							
7:00	GL (O)	GL (O)	GL (O)	GL (O)	GL (O)	GL (O)	GL (O)	GL (O)
7:05	GL (D)	GL (D)	GL (D)	GL (D)	GL (D)	GL (D)	GL (D)	GL (D)
7:10	Team D							
7:30	Team O							
7:45	Team D							
8:00	Team O							
8:15	Condition							
	Lightning Period							
8:30	½ Gassers / Done							

Blocking and tackling with the head making the initial contact is illegal—don't do it!

Figure 7-2c: Sample Wednesday practice schedule.

TRITON FOOTBALL PRACTICE SCHEDULE

Pre Practice: None

Dress: Helmets and Shorts

Date: Thursday

Field: Main

T	QB'S	RB'S	WR'S	O LINE	D LINE	I LB	OLB	DB'S
12:45		Special Teams	Walk-Thru					
1:05		Special Teams	Script					
1:20	O Walk-Thru	O Walk-Thru	O Walk-Thru	O Walk-Thru	D Walk-Thru	D Walk-Thru	D Walk-Thru	D Walk-Thru
1:40	Team Meeting							
2:15	Done							

Blocking and tackling with the head making the initial contact is illegal—don't do it!

Figure 7-2d: Sample Thursday practice schedule.

EARLY OUTS

On Tuesdays and Wednesdays, an "Early Out" period is run for 15 minutes. During this time, all specialists are out returning punts and kicks, deep snapping, punting, kicking, and holding for field goals. All running backs and receivers are out doing "legsavers," a drill to catch the football without running complete routes. Each player is encouraged to catch the football at least seventy-five times during this period. This practice improves the pass-catching abilities of each receiver, which can translate into improved play execution.

OFFENSIVE IMPLEMENTATION (O IMPL.)

The "O Impl." (Offensive Implementation period) is where any new plays or concepts that need to be taught for that week are discussed with the entire offense and run against air. Game plans, tempos, new "series" (Chapter Nine), and any unique play adjustments to the No-Huddle are introduced at this time. This offensive period is practiced on Mondays only.

INDIVIDUALS (INDIV.)

Indiv. (Individuals) are fundamental techniques that need to be developed by each position and are practiced on a daily basis. No-Huddle has no impact whatsoever on this aspect of practice. These periods are run in the same way a "huddled" team would run them.

BLITZ WALK-THROUGH AND BLITZ PICK-UP

Blitz walk-through is run on Mondays, with the offense servicing themselves by setting up the opponent's defensive fronts, dogs, and blitzes so they can learn to recognize them. The starting quarterback, all running backs, and the offensive line are present during this period. This time is a strong teaching period, with no emphasis on tempo and No-Huddle repetition. On Wednesdays, blitz pickup is run in a No-Huddle format with a big emphasis on high reps and "coaching on the run" to increase the number of repetitions in practice. Coaching on the run is done by teaching kids while they are coming back to the line of scrimmage or, if the situation merits more time, pulling the player out of the drill and coaching him while another player is inserted in the drill during this brief period. The logistics of this drill call for the coach to stand behind the drill while yelling in the protection scheme (i.e. 5-step, 3-step pass, sprint-out, etc.). The defensive scout coach is given a sheet with the fronts, dogs, and blitzes to be run and told how many times to show each one (see Figure 7-4). The fronts and blitzes are run according to the number of times listed by each defensive look. If all of the blitzes are run in a drill, then the scout coach can run through them again for

EARLY OUTS
WR—Legsavers
QB/RB—Option Pitches
          —Check Down Passes

GL (O)
Inside Zone vs. (6-1 GL Man)
Spread Option
Special
Bootleg
39 (Fade)

TEAM O
Series
(2) Screens
(4) 5-Step Passes
(3) 3-Step Passes
(1) Bootleg
(2) Roll Out
(8) Runs
(2) Specials

O TEAM BLITZ
(Defense Checklist Given to Scout Coaches)
Rollout RT
Rollout LT
5-Step Pass 73
              75
              78
3-Step Pass 36
              39
              33
2 Screens
     —Explorer
     —Eagle

O RUN
Trap vs. 4-3
Draw Trap vs. 4-4
Counter Trey
Inside Reverse

1-ON-1 GL
Fade
Slant
Out
Burst
Comeback

INDIV
QB—WUÆSpecial Teams
Throw Receiver Routes
     Hitch
     Out
     Slant
     Go
     Option
     Choice
     Corner

SPECIAL SITUATIONS
(3)   3rd and 1-3
(4)   3rd and 4-6
(5)   3rd and 7-10

CONDITION—SCREENS/SPECIALS
Check Game Plan Sheet for List of All
Screens

SPECIAL TEAMS
Ghost Package
NOTES:

Figure 7-3: Sample Tuesday play checklist (written on the back of the practice schedule).

increased repetition and retention. Hand signals of common dogs, line stunts, and blitzes are sometimes used by the defensive scout coach to increase repetitions during this drill.

1-ON-1

The receivers are running 1-on-1 against the defensive secondary during this time on Mondays. In 1-on-1, route signals can be used for the receivers, but are not necessary. These hand signals between the receivers and the quarterback can increase repetitions in this drill. Consistent with the No-Huddle practice philosophy, one of the goals of this period is to get as many repetitions as possible. Goal line 1-on-1 is run on Tuesdays (see Figure 7-3 b) to simulate goal line pass defense. These man coverage periods are only run on Mondays and Tuesdays. The defense must be ready for as many repetitions as possible. Two coaches are used on both offense and defense. Receivers yell or signal the route to be run to the quarterback and the route is run quickly. Special attention is paid to matching player abilities to improve competition and performance.

OFFENSIVE SKELLY (O SKELLY)

During "O Skelly," the No-Huddle practice is different from that of "huddled" teams. The coach stands near the sideline to simulate the distance from which a signal is given. This stance is used throughout the spring, summer, and fall during skelly to improve signal recognition and tempo capabilities, and increase players' attention. During this period, the coach will teach his players by moving toward the drill after the signal has been made. This drill is a teaching period, but the goal is to still have all coaches coach on the run. The ball is moved from hash to hash as the completion or incompletion dictates. The coach has a "play checklist" to determine if all of the pass plays have been called during that period. This checklist is written on the back of each day's practice plan for easy access. For a 20-minute skelly, 30 to 40 plays are usually executed. On Mondays, during the offensive skelly, the offensive line and a couple of running backs are used to service the defense in a "run" period.

To facilitate maximum reps during "O Skelly," the defensive scout coach is given a list of coverages with the number of times each coverage is to be run (Figure 7-5).

On Sunday, the offensive coordinator will discuss special position techniques and defensive schemes that the opponent employs with the defensive scout coach to ensure the adjustments will be implemented. The defensive scout coaches will also watch film of the opponent to get a "feel" for the defense. Pass skelly is not run every day because it is unrealistic for the quarterback in terms of throwing the football. The quarterback should have a rush of defenders

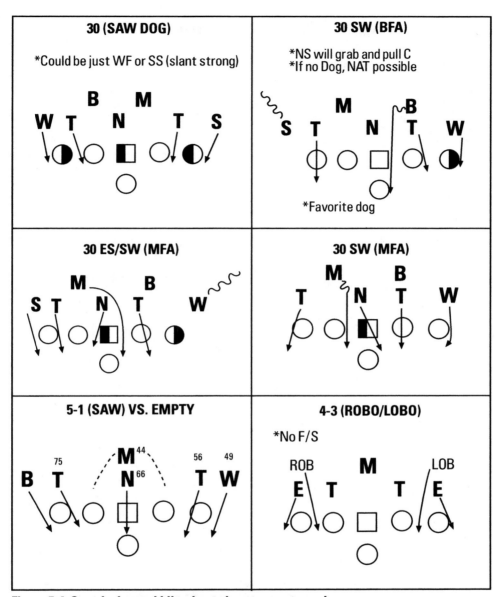

Figure 7-4: Sample dog and blitz sheet given to scout coaches.

COVERAGES	TIMES
2-Deep	10
3-Deep	15
Man Free	3
Man Blitz	2

Figure 7-5: Coverage checklist for 20-minute skelly for defensive scout coach.

to simulate game situations. On Tuesdays, skelly is run through a team blitz period that simulates defensive pressure and will be discussed later. On Wednesdays, a "Green Skelly" is run to simulate passing in the defensive red zone. This period warrants vital emphasis since scoring in the red zone often correlates to offensive success and a team victory. Red zone is a defensive term symbolizing stopping the offense in this area. The green zone is an offensive term for this area and tells the offense to go, go, go and score; thus a green zone attitude must be developed. On Wednesdays, during this period, the offensive line services the first defense in a "line stunt" period.

OFFENSIVE RUN (O RUN)

In the "O Run" period on Mondays, the following runs are practiced: inside and outside zone, speed option, and draw. These runs are signaled to the quarterback and the No-Huddle is always used. After each play, the players always go back to the line of scrimmage and wait for the next play to be called, with the offensive line in their "ready" position with their elbows on their knees. This system cuts down on the considerable amount of time used when players jog six yards to a huddle, jog back to the line of scrimmage, and then begin the cadence. In this 20-minute period, approximately 30 repetitions are accomplished against various fronts. The defensive scout coach is given a page of diagrams of the opponent's defensive fronts (see Figure 7-6). To increase offensive reps, he meets with the defensive scout players before practice begins to show the fronts to be run.

During this period, coaches are allowed to coach at a regular pace, but high repetitions are still encouraged. Each play is run against the prospective fronts in succession to increase retention of the blocking scheme before moving on to the next play. For example, an "inside zone" is run against a 4-3, then a 4-4, and then a 3-4 before running an "outside zone." Teams will often limit their fronts, dogs, and blitzes against a No-Huddle style, which reduces the number of repetitions needed in a run period. Playing against base fronts can improve play retention and enhance play execution; furthermore, the increased number of repetitions can be utilized to improve play execution.

In the "O run" period on Tuesdays, the following runs are practiced: inside trap, draw trap, counter trey, and any other special runs. All of the runs are also practiced within every team period as shown in the sample checklist for each practice day (see Figure 7-1). The first team period on Wednesday is an "all run" period and consists of a combination of different plays already practiced earlier in the week against different fronts and coverages.

TEAM PERIODS

The team period is always performed with a coaching on the run philosophy and is coupled with a goal of high repetitions against base fronts. In this 15-minute period, approximately 20 to 30 repetitions are achieved. Two defensive scout coaches coordinate the defensive scout team. The front must match the coverage in all situations. One of the defensive coaches is given the number of times the fronts/coverage should be seen in each period and an offensive assistant is given the offensive "play checklist" to make sure all plays planned to be run are practiced (see Figure 7-1). The coach still stands to the side to signal in all plays and then moves closer after the signal is completed to coach players.

During all team periods, the players are told to hustle back to the line of scrimmage and get in position for the next play to be called. The linemen are in the "ready" position waiting for the call and the receivers are in position to watch for the formation signal. After the play has been called, the linemen can make their split adjustments and the receivers should be set before the cadence begins. Linemen should be in a "set" position, which is with their hand on the ground ready to go, right after the play has been called and before the cadence begins. During most team periods, the ball is only moved from hash to hash depending upon the previous play to simulate "real game" circumstances. The ball is usually only moved down the field during "tempo" periods. During these team periods, it is extremely important that the defense get lined up as soon as the offense is aligned to allow the coach to make the call. Each team period focuses on different "play checklists" to practice the entire offensive package during each week.

CONDITIONING

The conditioning attitude begins in the spring, when every practice ends with intense conditioning. These intense conditioning periods continue through the summer to build a strong foundation and attitude for the season. The entire team must "buy into" the fact that a No-Huddle offense is really a No-Huddle team in terms of conditioning and the increased number of plays in each game.

The conditioning periods change each day. The theory behind changing the conditioning workouts and conditioning times is an effort to make this period as game-like as possible and to change the routine to reduce the risk of boredom and poor effort. The No-Huddle team must pride themselves on being highly conditioned and pay attention to this aspect of football throughout each practice. On Mondays, all players will run 10 40's at the end of practice. On Tuesdays, the offense will run all screens and specials against "air" at the 20-yard line, then

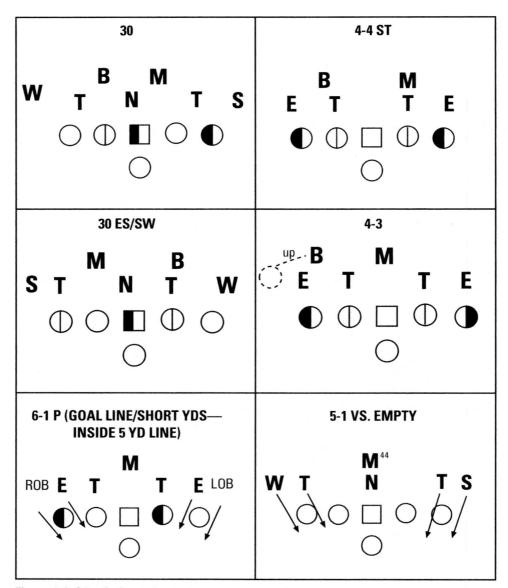

Figure 7-6: Sample front sheet given to scout coach.

sprint 20 yards, jog back 20, and get set again. This conditioning period has really improved the timing of screens and specials and allowed the offense to condition in a fun and productive way during the middle of practice (see Figure 7-2 b). The defense runs a pursuit drill during this time to improve angles and conditioning.

On Wednesdays, a "Lightning" period is run at the end of practice with the first offense and defense to simulate an Up tempo offense (Chapter Nine). The players run a team period of Up tempo offense non-stop for 15 minutes. All players not in the drill are running half-gassers at the other end of the field. On Thursdays, conditioning is not done at all so the players' legs are fresh on Friday night. On Saturdays, or the day following a game, the players jog for 20 minutes prior to watching films to loosen up any soreness and to maintain the strong aerobic foundation that has been developed in the summer. This exercise also provides for enhanced work-related recovery after each play during a game. Additionally, each practice is already laced with fast-paced work and increased repetitions to enhance conditioning.

O TEAM BLITZ

This period is a combination of blitz pick up and skelly and is only run on Tuesdays. The quarterback is put in a position where he must throw the football under pressure. If a team considers itself a passing team, the quarterback should be put in game-like situations in practice. For example, the quarterback should be throwing in drills and practice periods when the defense is moving toward him. Throwing the football without pressure (i.e., skelly) could give the quarterback a false sense of security in the pocket and reduce his ability to concentrate on his read progression with defenders moving toward him during a game.

In this period, the defense will run dogs, line stunts, and blitzes over 90 percent of the time. Coaching on the run is utilized again in this No-Huddle period. The two defensive scout coaches must be well-coordinated to make sure the correct front and coverage are run at a fast pace. This time is basically a "team" period which focuses on the blitz. It is an extremely important period used to simulate game situations at game speed.

GOAL LINE OFFENSE

Goal line offense is run twice a week in a down/distance (short yardage plays), "play checklist" format. The same No-Huddle format is run; however, in the goal line period, tempo is not as important and teaching becomes the highest priority. Plays can be stopped to teach the correct technique, method, and/or scheme. The coach should memorize basic short yardage personnel groups, formations, and plays by the end of each week through the use of the "play checklist" system.

LIGHTNING PERIOD

Every Wednesday, a "Lightning" period is run at the end of practice. This Up-tempo period pits the first team defense against the first team offense. The offensive skill players have wristbands that they refer to after a number is signaled in by the coach (see Chapter Nine for a complete description of how this tempo is executed). This 15-minute period is run with the coach on the sideline to create game-like conditions. The defense is allowed to run their scheme, but they can not run blitzes that will not be seen by the offense on Friday. This period is mainly an offensive period with great conditioning for the defense and an excellent way for the defense to prepare to face a two-minute offense.

WALK-THROUGH

In this style of offense, the tempo is often a vital component of success. The four-wide receiver offense can be very complicated; therefore, an offensive walk-through and discussion take place every week on Thursday. This period gives players a chance to ask questions and to be quizzed by the coach. The entire game plan, including each play, tempo, series, fronts, coverages, and blitzes, will be discussed thoroughly and walked through.

The mental side of the game is extremely important and each aspect of the plan is thoroughly covered. On Fridays (game day), each player is given a written test by his position coach that covers the items he needs to know for each game. These tests are corrected and reviewed with each player by the coaches approximately two hours before the game to ensure optimum mental preparation.

SATURDAYS

Saturdays are a review of the game on Friday night. The practice begins with a stretching period and then a 20-minute jog as described earlier. This period is followed with approximately one and a half hours of film of the game the night before. This film session is an extremely important part of the teaching process. Each play is reviewed comprehensively, with the focus on learning from the film to become better football players.

SPECIAL SITUATIONS

Many special situations can occur during a football game: third down situational plays, coming out plays, green zone plays, last three plays (to win), two-minute offense, four-minute offense, etc. All of these situations should be practiced in No-Huddle. The "play checklists" can be prepared to practice all third down plays during normal team periods with the appropriate fronts and coverages. The coach may identify a "team period" during the week that will be for all third down situations with the appropriate anticipated fronts and coverages run during this period. All other special situations are practiced within individual team periods with the appropriate defense called. For example, "coming out" plays and "last three" plays are practiced on Wednesday in the second team period (see Figure 7-2 c); the green zone offense is practiced during green skelly and goal-line periods; the two-minute offense is practiced in the Lightning period on Wednesday evening; and the four-minute offense is practiced early in the season and then just reviewed during walk-throughs on Thursdays.

SCOUT TEAM MANAGEMENT

In the No-Huddle, the scout team can really make a big difference in offensive success. The scout team coaches meet with the offensive coaches for a half-hour on Sundays and view film to understand the defensive schemes. The scout team coaches must educate the scout defensive personnel on Monday before practice to achieve the best look possible during practice. Players must align quickly and pay close attention to the scout coaches for optimal success during each period.

TWO-WAY PLAYERS

Each practice is set up as a two-platoon practice; however, the two-way players are discussed among the coaches for defensive or offensive practice priority for that season, week, and/or day. Depending upon the week, a two-way player may be focused on one side of the ball more than the other. Each two-way player already has an offensive or defensive priority, but the opponent, personnel injuries and the game plan for that week may change the priority of each two-way player in practice. Coaches must communicate before practice where two-way players will be during each drill to ensure optimum game preparation.

OPPOSING TEAM DEFENSIVE PRACTICE

The No-Huddle style is very difficult to simulate in practices for opposing defenses. They will usually waste valuable practice and meeting preparation time finding ways to imitate the No-Huddle and thus reduce the amount of time preparing to defend the offensive scheme. It is very difficult for a coach to define for his players the different tempos that can be run by a No-Huddle team. Simulating the tempos in practice with a scout team is even more difficult. Some coaches have run two sets of receivers and running backs to simulate the tempo speed; however, to maintain the tempo, the scout coaches can not really coach when the scout team players make mistakes on scheme, making it even more difficult to run the No-Huddle tempo. Because it can be more stressful and frustrating for the coach to practice against the No-Huddle, the anxiety levels rise for coaches, scout players, and defensive players during the week of practice. Practice preparation could also increase for the defensive coaches when they make twice the number of practice cards for the two groups of scout players. Additionally, identifying twice the number of scout players that will give a "good look" to the defense might be difficult. Conditioning for the No-Huddle has proven to be extremely tough for a team accustomed to the regular number of plays per game. These items all help give an advantage to the No-Huddle style.

Key Coaching Points in a No-Huddle Practice

The following points should be addressed when running a No-Huddle practice:

→ Maintain tempos.

→ Condition hard.

→ Develop a well-conditioned attitude among players.

→ Keep defensive terminology the same on both sides of the ball for easier alignment and adjustments to enhance practice pace and execution.

→ Prepare scout coaches and players.

→ Always use signals and No-Huddle in practices.

→ Test players on terms and signals often and early.

→ Lightning cards and series should be introduced every Monday.

→ Practice Lightning each week.

→ Practice "Series" twice a week.

→ Develop "play checklists" for every situation.

→ Players should hustle back to the line of scrimmage every time.

→ Coach on the run.

The No-Huddle offense can be practiced in a normal practice structure with just a few exceptions. The placing of the coach, tempos in practice, conditioning focus, "play checklists," and coaching philosophy in practice are a few areas that the coach will need to adjust to fit the No-Huddle style. These small practice adaptations are very minor compared to the big adjustments that the opposing defenses must make in order to be competitive with the No-Huddle. In relation to practice, the No-Huddle style affords a major advantage in terms of play repetition and conditioning, creating opponent anxiety, and the disruption of an opponent's practice structure.

CHAPTER 8

GAME PLANNING AND GAME EXECUTION

Preparation for a game in the No-Huddle style is very similar to the preparation of a team that huddles. In game preparation, the major considerations still tend to be the offensive scheme in relationship to the opponent's defense and personnel match-ups. In this chapter, the three main factors in preparing for a football game will be addressed: (1) game planning, (2) game management, and (3) game mechanics. Basic items in each of these three phases of offensive football fundamental components will be discussed with special attention focused on the No-Huddle style.

GAME PLANNING

Typically, at the high school level, game planning begins on Saturday with the viewing of the opponent's film. The offense will usually view as much film as is available. The staff will typically look for specific types of things as the offensive scheme dictates. The following is a brief list of typical items offensive coaches are looking for when viewing film for any type of offense:

→ Fronts

→ Coverages

→ Dogs/Blitzes used

→ Down/Distance tendencies

→ Defensive formation tendencies

→ Hash tendencies

→ Personnel

→ Substitution patterns

→ Unique defensive alignments and techniques used.

→ Defense in the red zone (I believe this area should be called the green zone to remind the offense to go, go, go)

→ Defense coming out

→ Defense after a big play or turnover.

→ "Opening" defenses

In the No-Huddle style, it is also important ask the following questions:

→ How many two-way players do they have and what positions do they play?

→ Does the defense like to disguise coverages?

→ Are they a better team than we are?

→ Is their offense good?

→ Is their offense wide open or ball-control oriented?

→ Are they well-coached?

→ Are they lazy?

→ Are they well-conditioned?

→ Is it early in the season?

→ Is this a new opponent?

Many teams will address the above items according to their offensive schematic needs. In the remainder of this chapter the No-Huddle style will be discussed in relationship to the four-wide receiver offense that is run at San Clemente High School, with special attention given to the above questions.

The number of two-way players of an opponent can determine how much Up-tempo (Chapter Nine) offense should be run to fatigue the opposition and force them to use less talented players. If a team completely two-platoons, running Up-tempo should be discussed among the staff to determine if it would give the offense an advantage. Even if a team two-platoons, Up-tempo can give the offense an advantage as a momentum shifter, limit defensive substitutions, and restrict the defense from disguising coverages. This strategy forces a complex defensive team to simplify, thereby making them more predictable. Additionally, although many two-way skill players can handle a No-Huddle pace, two-way linemen have difficulty. Therefore, if a team has two-way players up front, the No-Huddle attack could severely affect the opponent.

The No-Huddle can slow down just as easily as it speeds up. If an opposing team is significantly better than his own, a coach can slow the game down to decrease the number of plays in an attempt to keep the game close. In 1995, when San Clemente defeated the defending national champions, Mater Dei, the game plan was to slow the tempo down to keep the game close with the hope of having a chance to win in the fourth quarter. The plan was successful. If the opponent's offense is extremely talented, the objective might be to keep them off of the field by slowing the tempo down. If their offense is average or poor, a No-Huddle team might want to increase the tempo early and try to develop a quick lead to get a ball control-type team out of its comfort zone. The choices and options for handling an opponent with the No-Huddle are unlimited.

Teams that are well-coached are usually in the correct position when the play begins. Therefore, most teams will align and show the offense what scheme they are in. Lazy teams or teams that are not well-conditioned can be hurried with Up tempo early to increase the possibility of fatigue. In fact, early in the year, No-Huddle teams can gain a great advantage against poorly-conditioned teams. Whatever the situation, the coach must make some solid decisions about the best way to attack an opponent using the No-Huddle offense.

Once all of the questions have been answered regarding an upcoming opponent, a coach can implement his game plan for the week. As discussed in the previous chapter, he should make sure that the plays that will be run on Friday night are practiced efficiently during the week. Some teams do not do a good job of practicing the game plan during the week. Each week, the No-Huddle game plan should always include all three tempos even if they may not all be run.

Game plans must be well-thought out and developed in a consistent and thorough manner. In Brian Billick's book, *Developing an Offensive Game Plan*, he discussed many factors related to implementing a successful game plan. Topics included how much offense to install, how to prepare the amount of offense to run, game-plan preparation, and many others. He believes in developing the offense according to situations and identifying the plays to be run in certain circumstances in the staff meetings early in the week. In the No-Huddle offense, the plays are written on the game plan forms shown in Figure 8-1. The plays are listed according to special situations, defensive coverages, down and distance, and formations. This form was developed from a combination of those that have been used over the years by various teams. The plays are written on the game plan sheets at the beginning of each week under the appropriate category. During the week of practice, some plays may be eliminated and others adjusted slightly. These game plan sheets are read and re-read prior to each game for higher retention by the coach. They are placed back to back in a plastic cover for protection and easier accessibility during a game.

San Clemente has four offensive varsity coaches. Most of them teach full-time; therefore, they have very little time in the week to prepare for an opponent. On Saturday, the staff works until about five o'clock to break down film and review the previous game. On Sunday, the offensive staff meets for approximately five hours to prepare the game plan and put the offensive scouting report together. The staff does not meet again until Friday just prior to the game, unless the need arises at some point during the week. High school coaches should realize that the No-Huddle can be run without a great deal of preparation time and meetings. How the No-Huddle is used on game night is usually predicated upon game-management information acquired from the offensive assistants before and during the game progression.

PLAY SHEET

Categorize by formation and/or motions

Runs	3-Step	5-Step	Play Pass	Goal Line Package

Coverages

0	5	51	1	11 (Man Blitz)	4 (Bracket)

Screens	Draws	Dash Rt/Lt	Ghost	Sprint Rt/Lt

Runs

Hit Chart

○ ○ ○ □ ○ ○ ○

Figure 8-1a: Sample No-Huddle game plan sheet.

First 15 Plays		Kill Clock Runs		Notes
		Kill Clock Time		
		Officials' Names		

3rd (1-3)	3rd (4-6)	3rd (7+)	Short Ydg	2nd (1-3)
2 Pt. Plays	Up Tempo	Snake Eyes (after a big turnover)	3 Plays to Win	Full Protect

Specials	+20	+10	+5	-10

Figure 8-1b: Sample No-Huddle game plan sheet.

GAME MANAGEMENT

The No-Huddle style is a flexible system of offense that will usually take advantage of a defense based upon a coach's game management situations. During a game, the coach will ask the assistants for specific information regarding personnel, defensive schemes, and many other items that are important to getting the most out of the No-Huddle. In order to obtain this information as it unfolds during a game, the following items need to be addressed: offensive assistants' game responsibilities, defensive schemes, tempos, and game plan implementation.

The offensive assistants look for many items that are scheme specific. In this style of offense, down and distance situations are not quite as important as defensive scheme identification unless there are specific scheme tendencies according to down and distance. The coach can usually identify fronts and/or coverages (usually base defenses) early and make a play selection based upon what would be the most successful against the defense shown. For example, in a four-wide receiver offense, if the secondary is playing two-deep five-under zone, the defense has only five players in the box (between the tackles). Therefore, the offense should run the ball more often to take advantage of the defensive scheme.

Many times a No-Huddle team can get aligned quickly and force the defense to line up. The coach can then make a play selection based upon what front and coverage the defense is in. If teams can align quickly, the coach can completely control the game tempo and make optimum play choices. A coach could also get the offense set in a formation quickly, motion a player to change the formation, and then "freeze" the offense to see how the defense adjusted to the formation. He would then call the play based upon the defense scheme. The offensive assistants are also charting each play on a spreadsheet (see Figure 8-2) to discover any tendencies the defense has and to determine the plays that have been the most successful in the game up to that point.

Between each series, an offensive assistant will tally the plays and write the pertinent information on a tendency sheet (see Figure 8-3). The coach can use this sheet to identify tendencies and make the appropriate offensive adjustments.

Tempos can have a dramatic effect on game management The next chapter contains a complete discussion on the use of tempos. If a team has built a lead or the pace needs to be slowed down considerably, the Slow tempo is implemented. An assistant coach stands next to the coach calling plays and he watches the official chopping the football into play. Once the ball has been chopped, he starts a stopwatch. The play is signaled in, but the quarterback does not start the cadence until the coach points at him, usually with about five seconds left before a delay of game is called. This strategy allows for maximum use of the clock on every down. This tempo can also be used to disrupt the rhythm of an explosive opposing offense.

SC VS. _____									
SER	D/D	HASH	FORM	PLAY	DEFENSE	COVERAGE	LINE STUNTS	DOGS	BLITZES	GAIN	COMMENTS

Figure 8-2: Game charting sheet.

OFFENSIVE SUMMARY SHEET		
FRONTS	**STUNTS/DOGS/BLITZES**	**COVERAGES**
1st and 10		
2nd and 9+ yds		
2nd and 4-8 yds		
2nd and 1-3 yds		
3rd and 10+ yds		
3rd and 4-9 yds		
3rd (4th) and 1-3 yds		

Figure 8-3: Defensive tendency sheet.

Signaling in the play may be the most important part of the communication process. If the play is signaled in incorrectly, the wrong play is called, reducing offensive success. Therefore, in this style of communication, the offensive coordinator signals in all plays and accepts full responsibility for any mistake that occurs. It is hard to signal plays when holding a game plan, so he should decide where to keep the game plan when signaling. Some coaches clip the plan onto a belt loop and let it dangle in front of them. Some put the plan in their back pocket and refer to it during time-outs or between series. The bottom line is that the hands need to be free to signal and the plan needs to be kept in a consistent place. If the game plan is written, practiced, read, re-read, and edited (if necessary), the coach should have a good idea of what the plan is. If the coach is trying to maintain a certain game pace or is given too many choices in a critical situation, it is difficult to consult a game plan. Therefore, in this style, the game plan should be somewhat memorized during the week and only referred to during time-outs and between series.

GAME MECHANICS

The mechanics of signaling and executing a play will be explored in this section. Many factors affect how formations, motions and plays are signaled; however, the greatest factor is the tempo being used. Chapter Nine provides a complete description of tempo use and mechanics. In the following discourse, several key coaching points for communicating the No-Huddle offense in a football game will be discussed.

At the beginning of each series, the team will huddle approximately six yards from the line of scrimmage. The reasons for huddling up at this time are: (1) to relay any important information and adjustments to two-way players, (2) to establish an "attitude" for the series about to be run, and (3) for the quarterback to relay any reminders from the coach.

As discussed earlier, the offensive coordinator will signal in all of the plays. He should wear a shirt that is a color opposite that of the team's jerseys so he can be seen more readily. For example, if the team is in light jerseys, he should wear a dark shirt. All skill players should look at the coach immediately following a play for the signal for the next formation and/or play. After the receivers have looked, they must make sure that they are within fifteen yards of the ball before the ball is snapped; otherwise a penalty could be assessed.

Tempo affects how plays are signaled, but the following scenario of game mechanics is a typical progression of a No-Huddle play run in the regular tempo. All skill players look at the offensive coordinator for the formation and possible motion signals. Once the signals have been made, the quarterback, who is three to five yards from the line of scrimmage, cups his hands over his mouth and yells the signal to all of the offense both ways. After identifying the defense, the coach will signal in the play. The receivers might adjust their alignments while the quarterback is yelling the play to all of the players. Once the play has been signaled in, all players should be in their "set" position before the cadence begins, including the offensive linemen. These players are bent over with their elbows on their thighs so that the defense will align and the coach can see the defensive scheme. The quarterback yells the play to the left and the right every time to let the offensive line know the play and for any skill player who may have missed the signal for whatever reason. The quarterback is five yards from the line of scrimmage while yelling the signals, to make sure the entire offense can hear him and for better coverage recognition. One disadvantage of this alignment is that the defense may not get set until the quarterback puts his hands underneath the center. However, the shotgun formation is used often in this offensive scheme, forcing teams to be aligned and ready to play at all times. After everybody is set to go, the cadence begins "set, hut, hut, hut."

In the final analysis, for an offense to be successful, careful game planning, effective game management, and efficient game mechanics must be executed. The No-Huddle style adds another dimension that the defense must prepare for, thus decreasing the amount of time focused on defending the offensive scheme. The No-Huddle offense is an explosive and innovative offensive style that can only enhance offensive production when run effectively.

CHAPTER 9

NO-HUDDLE TEMPOS

Game tempos can have a major impact on the outcome of a football game. Since tempo is such an important factor, the coach should try to control this aspect of the game. Tempos can help an offensive coach dictate opposing defensive schemes, defensive personnel, and game momentum. By running the No-Huddle style of offense, the coach can completely control the tempo of the entire game. In fact, in many cases, the tempo fluctuations in the No-Huddle style not only destroy the opponents' defensive rhythm, but can push opposing offenses into the same hurried rhythm as the No-Huddle team. This change often causes anxiety and confusion among opposing offenses and offensive coaching staffs. The changing rhythm and Up tempo can create severe problems for the defense. In this chapter, three tempos will be discussed in depth, with special attention being made to why, when, and how you run these tempos; these tempos are Slow, Regular, and Up tempo. Some other special tempo changers, such as running a series, "alerts," and using the quarterback sneak as a weapon, will also be explained.

SLOW TEMPO

→ **Why?**

⇒ To keep a game close when playing a better team.

⇒ To change game momentum.

⇒ To give rest to two-way players.

⇒ The coach can identify fronts and coverages for better play selection.

⇒ The offense runs check-with-me's at the line of scrimmage.

→ **When?**

⇒ If a team builds a lead and wants to control the clock.

⇒ At the very beginning of the game, to set the tempo and frustrate the defense.

⇒ Immediately following an Up-tempo period when the defense is in a habit of aligning quickly for better defensive scheme recognition.

→ How?

⇒ One or two coaches can signal in the formation and possibly the motion.

⇒ Entire offense aligns and gets in stances quickly.

⇒ Coach checks defensive fronts, coverages, and alignments.

⇒ Based on above information, the coach signals in the best play against the defensive scheme, alignment, or personnel.

⇒ An assistant coach must have stopwatch going when the ball is chopped for play to reduce the risk of delay of game penalties.

⇒ Play is executed two seconds before a delay of game penalty is assessed to maximize the amount of time used.

→ Key Coaching Points:

⇒ Come up with names for various tempos so players know which tempo is being used.

⇒ Dummy signals must be used if the defense begins to pick up No-Huddle communication.

⇒ Practice aligning quickly to get the desired defensive look.

⇒ Make sure all offensive personnel align quickly to improve play selection.

⇒ Realize the defense can substitute in this tempo.

⇒ Understand the defense can disguise and stem in this tempo.

⇒ Run after Up tempo to get defense in rhythm of aligning quickly.

⇒ To slow down the game after a lead is built (i.e. four-minute offense), have an assistant watch the ball being chopped and start his clock. Signal in the play and point to the quarterback when it is time to begin the cadence (usually at 20 seconds).

Teams may have many reasons for slowing the tempo down, but the predominant one is generally to gain an advantage by identifying the defensive scheme. In a four-wide receiver offensive scheme, the defensive shell (coverage alignment) is usually given away in this tempo. As shown below, the defensive coverage can impact the type of pass that an offense would use to attack a particular coverage. Even though the passing game has progressed to where receivers adjust routes according to the coverage after the snap of the ball, some pass plays are better against certain type of coverages. For example, a vertical stretch concept is best against two-deep, five-under zone coverage

(Diagram 9-1 a and b), while a horizontal stretch is best against a three-deep four-under zone coverage (Diagram 9-2). These coverages are easily identifiable during this tempo, thus maximizing the coach's ability to call the best possible play against the defense shown.

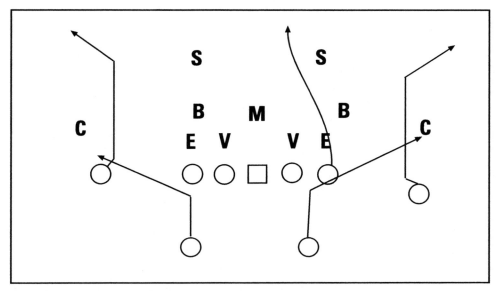

Diagram 9-1a: Vertical stretch vs. two-deep five-under zone coverage.

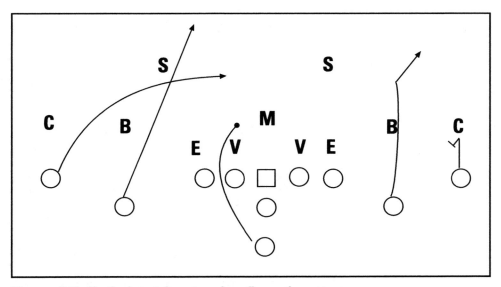

Diagram 9-1b: Vertical stretch vs. two-deep five-under zone coverage.

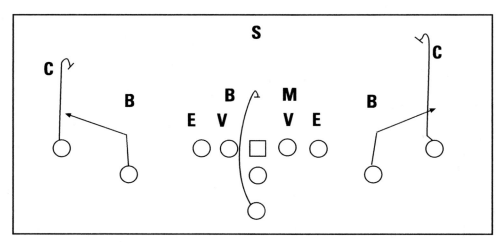

Diagram 9-2: Horizontal stretch vs. three-deep four-under zone.

The run game can also be enhanced by front recognition. Many teams will run check-with-me's at the line of scrimmage and can not run the play unless the defense aligns to determine the direction of the play. If the offense slows down the tempo after Up tempo, the defense will still be forced to align quickly, thus giving the quarterback a better opportunity to identify the run direction. If check-with-me's are not a part of the offensive package, then front recognition might be critical in establishing the best run call. In a college 4-3, the inside zone would be best when called away from the extra linebacker (Diagram 9-3). The inside trap is best run toward a "3" technique (Diagram 9-4). When the offense is aligned quickly, the defense must also get aligned, thus increasing the chances of making the right play selection. A coach may look for any number of things in order to correctly identify fronts and coverages and, subsequently, select the appropriate play.

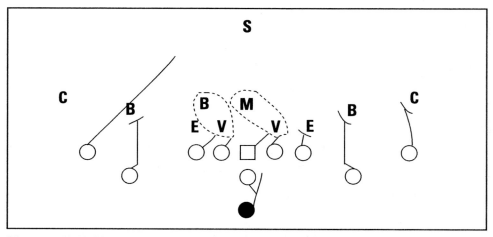

Diagram 9-3: Inside zone run away from the extra linebacker.

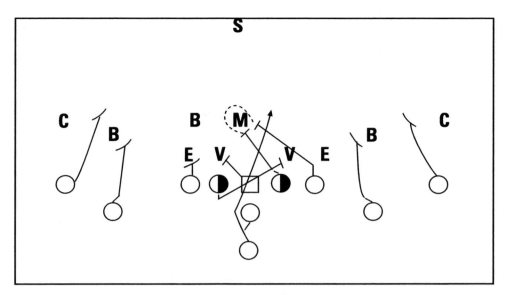

Diagram 9-4: Inside trap vs. "3" technique.

In the passing game, mismatches in personnel are often easier to identify in this tempo, and therefore can be capitalized upon. A slower linebacker versus the best receiver or a small cornerback against a tall receiver can be personnel situations to take advantage of. Defenses will often substitute in slow tempo, making it easier to identify personnel and schematic weaknesses to exploit. Whatever the case, the slow tempo can give the offense another big advantage in moving the football and scoring points.

REGULAR TEMPO

The regular tempo is run in a manner similar to the slow tempo with a few exceptions. The coach can signal the formation and the play at the same time. He could also continue to signal formations and then identify fronts and/or coverages and make his play selection. If teams are staying in base fronts and coverages, which happens often, the coach has already identified the defensive scheme and can make play selections more quickly. Many teams like to stay in base defenses so the players are not caught out of position when the play begins. The regular tempo is the base style of No-Huddle play in which the coach controls the tempo and rhythm of the game.

→ **Why?**

⇒ Establishes a "normal" game rhythm.

⇒ The coach can identify fronts and coverages for better play selection.

⇒ The offense runs check-with-me's at the line of scrimmage.

→ When?

⇒ At the very beginning of the game to set the tempo and frustrate the defense.

⇒ The defense is sitting in a base front and/or coverage nearly all of the time.

⇒ When a coach wants to maintain a "normal" game rhythm.

→ How?

⇒ Huddle at the beginning of each series to get information to two-way players and/or to establish a series attitude and goal.

⇒ One or two coaches can signal in the formation, motion and possibly the play.

⇒ All players must be within 15 yards of the ball when it is chopped into play.

⇒ The quarterback, running backs, and receivers must be looking at the coach for signals.

⇒ The quarterback is three to five yards from the center when calling formations, motion, plays and cadence.

⇒ Entire offense aligns and gets in stances quickly.

⇒ Coach could check defensive fronts, coverages and alignments.

⇒ Play is then executed.

→ Key Coaching Points:

⇒ Practice at the pace expected in game.

⇒ Have a game plan ready for attacking base defenses in Regular tempo.

⇒ The quarterback must look at coach for a second longer in case the entire play is signaled in with the formation.

⇒ Linemen must have their hands or elbows on their thighs ready to go ("Ready" position). Linemen make alignment adjustments in "Ready" position.

⇒ Only coaching on the run is allowed during tempo and team periods.

⇒ Dummy signals must be used if defense begins to pick up No-Huddle communication.

⇒ Practice aligning quickly to get the desired defensive look.

⇒ Make sure all offensive personnel align quickly to improve your play selection.

⇒ Understand the defense can disguise and stem in this tempo.

⇒ Can run after up tempo to get defense in rhythm of aligning quickly.

The regular tempo of No-Huddle offense is the most often-used tempo. With this tempo in place, an average team will run approximately 20-25 percent more plays in a football game than a team that huddles up. This change in game rhythm will usually keep a defense in base fronts and coverages with very little personnel substitution, allowing the offensive coach to dictate the game tempo, defensive scheme and personnel. Some teams like to disguise coverages, stem their defensive fronts, and substitute freely. The No-Huddle style can respond to this strategy by going to up-tempo offense.

UP TEMPO

This tempo is completely different from the other two. When executed correctly, it can really put pressure on the defense. Up tempo is a scheme that emphasizes high percentage plays that can be run against any front or coverage and at an extremely fast rate. This tempo will usually get the same defensive look for each play because of the hurried pace. Each week the staff should decide which plays to include against whatever defense you expect to see in this situation. Many times defenses will not even be aligned when the ball is snapped.

→ **Why?**

⇒ Defensive front stems frequently.

⇒ Defense likes to disguise the coverage.

⇒ The defense will not align to give the offense an advantage.

⇒ To kick-start the offense and change the momentum of the game.

⇒ The offense has to score immediately.

⇒ To develop confidence in the offense to be able to score quickly and at will.

⇒ The two-minute offense is routine (no anxiety when put in this situation).

⇒ To set a frenzied pace from the beginning of the game and increase anxiety among the opposing defense.

→ When?

⇒ At the beginning of the game or second half.

⇒ At the end of the half to score quickly.

⇒ The team is behind and must score.

⇒ To produce quick points and establish offensive confidence and dominance early.

⇒ After slow tempo to change the momentum.

⇒ Before slow tempo to get the defense to align quicker.

Many teams have their own method for a two-minute offense. Some teams will have a specific group of plays that they run, while others will have an elaborate non-verbal signal system to execute a diverse number of plays. In the following discussion of how to run the up-tempo offense, the details of how San Clemente executes this pace will be disclosed. This approach may not be the best way for every team to run this tempo, but we decided after many hours of discussion and many game mistakes that it was the best approach for San Clemente.

→ How?

⇒ Keep this tempo simple with high percentage plays.

⇒ Use only one formation (can be flopped) to keep it simple.

⇒ No formation call or cadence is ever needed in this tempo once initiated.

⇒ San Clemente can also sometimes insert an "empty" package in this tempo.

⇒ Never use motion.

⇒ Never use check-with-me's at the line of scrimmage.

⇒ Always go on the same count (i.e., first sound or one).

⇒ Get wristbands that have numbers next to the plays.

⇒ Group plays according to run, pass, or screen. Use highlighting for better differentiation between types of plays (see Figure 9-1).

⇒ Coach signals numbers using the body clock (review Chapter Five).

⇒ Players look to their wristbands immediately for the play (linemen do not have a wristband).

⇒ The play is next to the corresponding number that has been signaled in.

⇒ Receivers may adjust their alignments at this point, but must do so quickly.

⇒ Quarterback yells number and term to alert the linemen to what the play is.

⇒ Play is executed.

⇒ Players hustle to spot where next play is about to begin, while going through the same steps as previously listed.

→ **Key Coaching Points:**

⇒ Practice at least twice a week for 15 minutes against first defense.

⇒ Coach on the run for both sides of the ball during these periods.

⇒ Coaches can use plays that are not necessarily listed on the wristband.

⇒ All skill players must look at the coach immediately after the previous play for the next play, even if they are just getting off of the ground.

⇒ Keep the Up tempo package simple.

⇒ Make sure linemen are getting in their stance immediately.

⇒ Any penalty can ruin up tempo, so really preach discipline during this tempo.

⇒ Practice at the pace expected in the game.

⇒ A signal and term should be devised to stop this tempo at any time.

UP TEMPO MATER DEI	
Ghost R/L	**Right**
1. Levi 3	1. Denver
2. Levi 6	2. Explorer
3. Ocean	3. Levi 6
4. Pier	4. Levi 4
5. Switch	5. Beach
6. Nam 7	6. Ricky
7. Nam 8	7. Lucy
8. Man 9	8. Nam 8
9. Casper	9. Monarch

Table 9-1: Up Tempo card for wristband

The up-tempo aspect of the No-Huddle is designed to completely disrupt the rhythm of the game. This tempo can be used at the start of a game to establish offensive dominance, momentum and confidence. If a defense feels that a team can score quickly and at will, their confidence will drop and the offensive tempo can dictate the outcome of the game. If an opponent is young or lacking confidence because of recent game performances, the up tempo is a perfect way to start a game. This style of offense promotes offensive confidence, reduces offensive anxiety and establishes offensive control over the rhythm of the game.

SERIES

Running a "series" is an excellent way to change momentum and take control of the game. A series is a pre-determined package of three plays that is carefully designed according to predicted defensive schemes, hash tendencies and down/distance tendencies. This package is given the name of the opponent each week and is practiced five minutes each day in practice to ensure success on Friday night. The series is designed with the best plays in the offense or a series of similar action plays. The third play must be a play that is designed for third down and 6-10 yards to go. The series is run without a huddle and in up-tempo fashion, with the ball being snapped on the first sound. Check-with-me's are not used, but motion is sometimes used if the play dictates it. After the first play is run, the entire team hustles to the ball and the second play is run immediately. After the second play is executed, the team sprints to the ball and the third play is run. If the series is carefully designed, a first down is almost assured, with the offense subsequently developing some momentum and confidence. When designing a series, the coach should give careful consideration to hash position possibilities after each play. For example, a sweep right could put the offense on the right hash; therefore, the next play should be designed as a right hash play. Because the hash marks are closer to the boundary in high school, the coach should exhibit greater care in play selection on the hash. A series can be run more than once a game, but should be changed each week to eliminate tendencies. In three years of running series, San Clemente has achieved first downs 100 percent of the time. That is an incredible statistic. The series is an excellent way to start a game or second half to establish dominance and confidence. If developed and utilized properly, it can be a very powerful weapon in your No-Huddle arsenal of tempos.

ALERTS

Another tempo changer is an "alert" package. "Alerts" are used at any time and from any position on the field. They have proven to be especially successful in third down situations. "Alerts" are run at the fastest pace possible. Once the quarterback has yelled "alert," every player gets in his stance wherever he is aligned (offensive linemen should try to get toe to toe). The ball will be snapped on the first sound, so expedience in alignment is critical. The purpose of this scheme is to really catch the defense off guard, possibly even while they are still looking at their coach for the defensive call. "Alerts" have been very effective when run from regular or slow tempos when defenses take their time in getting aligned.

An "alert" package will usually consist of a quarterback sneak, a speed option, a "freeze" play and/or a special type of play. The quarterback sneak is an offensive weapon that is usually untapped. For the past two years, San Clemente has averaged over seven yards per carry on quarterback sneaks, which

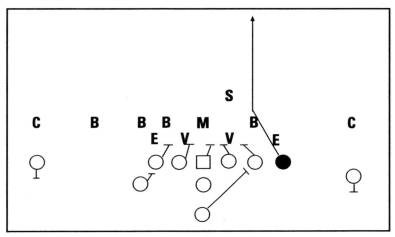

Diagram 9-5: Alert special—fake quarterback sneak and then throw to the tight end.

are usually run two to four times per game. The sneak is run in combination with the "alert," which usually catches defenses standing up and waiting for the defensive call. It is often used in critical 3rd-and-short situations and almost always results in a first down. The play is run quickly as described above, and the offensive line wedge blocks and stays low as the quarterback stays low and drives his legs. As mentioned earlier in the book, one sneak this past year went for eighty yards and a touchdown, while the entire defense was waiting for the defensive call.

Later in the year, the quick alignment of the "alert" often has defenses aligning quickly and condensing their defensive alignment near the center and linebackers, cheating forward to stop the sneak. When this situation occurs, the speed option is an outstanding adjustment. The tempo and urgency of the offense is the same as in all "alerts." The quarterback waits just a bit longer to snap the football to allow the defensive front seven to cheat to the center to stop the quarterback sneak. After the defense cheats toward the center, the ball is snapped and the speed option is run on the perimeter with no help from inside linebackers. This strategy has been a great scheme adjustment to take advantage of a defensive adjustment to a No-Huddle tendency.

Most teams run some sort of "freeze" play to draw a defense offside to get a first down. A "freeze" play can be run off the "alert" package. With the quick alignment of the "alert," most defenses have increased levels of anxiety and are anticipating a big offensive surge on the first sound. The quarterback yells "alert cube" (ice *cubes* are *freezing*), and the offense gets aligned. The quarterback waits a bit like he did in the speed option to allow the defense to align and then barks out a loud cadence to get the defense to come offside. If this attempt is unsuccessful, he yells "easy," and then calls the play to be executed. The No-Huddle allows more than enough time for all of these steps.

When running a No-Huddle style of offense, a coach can get very creative to take advantage of defenses. In an "alert" package, a special type of play may be practiced and run to take advantage of defensive alignments and tendencies. For example, a team might utilize a fake quarterback sneak and a pass to a tight end running through a linebacker. This play resulted in a long gain and a touchdown for Drew Bledsoe and Washington State against USC in a 4th-down-and-short situation (Diagram 9-5). The possibilities for creating offensive advantages by utilizing No-Huddle tempos are endless.

Tempos are at the heart of the No-Huddle style. The coach can influence the entire game by controlling its tempo. The No-Huddle style can give a team an incredible advantage when the tempos are used effectively.

CHAPTER 10

GO FOR IT

The No-Huddle is a unique and exciting offense that can really enhance offensive production in any offensive scheme. This book has covered some of the main aspects of the No-Huddle offense as it relates to the high school coach; however, a coach at any level who is interested in improving his offensive knowledge could benefit from this book. The ideas contained in this book are shared with the hope of opening the door to the No-Huddle system so that coaches can see for themselves what is inside. This chapter contains a summary of the information presented in this book, including a review of the reasons for running the No-Huddle.

At the beginning of Part I, Chapter One discussed a comprehensive view of why to run the No-Huddle. The reasons for running the No-Huddle are many and varied. One of the main reasons is that the offense will have improved play execution through increased practice repetitions and a decreased number of defensive looks. The coach can also control the game tempo and thereby affect the game rhythms, the defensive scheme, and an opponent's substitution patterns. The No-Huddle team is better conditioned on both sides of the ball and is used to the longer game. The opposing defense has a difficult time simulating the tempo in practice and may spend more time preparing for the No-Huddle tempo and less time preparing for the offensive scheme that is being run. The players like the "secret" language and are more motivated to practice at a faster pace in this exciting style of offense.

Chapters Two through Four contained complete descriptions of three No-Huddle systems. The systems are different from each other, but they still communicate the same information to the offense. Each system is run at a different level of competition (NFL, university, high school). Every system was explored using the same communication components and evaluated at the end of each chapter. These systems were introduced to show different ways that the No-Huddle could be implemented into any offensive scheme and provide some insight into how coaches devise systems of communication outside of the huddle.

At the end of Part I, Chapter Five explored a No-Huddle communication system in more depth. This system may not be the best to use for all offenses, but it has worked well for several high school programs that are currently employing this style. This system was explained beginning with the brainstorming process and progressing through the final product.

In Part II, the communication mechanics of the No-Huddle were discussed. Once the system has been decided upon, determining how to teach the system to the players is the next priority. Chapter Six presented the most effective methods for teaching the No-Huddle. The next chapter showed that the No-Huddle practice can be run in a manner very similar to a regular practice during the week. Only a few adaptations to the practice structure must be adhered to (i.e., the placement of the coach during drills when signaling plays, the tempos being practiced, and "play checklists" to ensure that the game plan is practiced during the week).

Chapter Eight discussed the No-Huddle game plan, game management, and game execution in depth. The No-Huddle game plan is similar to a regular game plan with just a few exceptions (i.e., questions regarding opposing two-way players must be addressed in order to determine what type of tempos will be used during the game, etc.). In game management, the assistant coaches can assist in front and coverage identification. This information, coupled with effective use of tempos, can enable the offensive coordinator to make the best possible play call on every down. Game execution was addressed from the signals to the team's execution. Each aspect of the mechanics of running a play was described to show how the offense is run during a game.

In Chapter Nine, the different tempos were described and evaluated. Many people believe the No-Huddle is a "hurry-up" offense all of the time; however, on the contrary, the No-Huddle offense can take as much time as the coach desires to run a play. The different tempos give the offense a distinct advantage. The coach can slow down to get a better view of the defensive scheme or to disturb the rhythm of an opponent's explosive offense. He could also speed up to change the momentum of a game, fatigue teams who have two-way players or are poorly-conditioned, or to make defenses align more quickly so he can get a better look at the front and coverage. After accomplishing this goal, he can then return to a slower tempo, if desired. For example, a team might be disguising their coverages or stemming their fronts and not aligning quickly. If the offense goes to the Up tempo, teams will get aligned more quickly and get used to that rhythm. Even after the No-Huddle coach returns to a slower tempo, the defense will still align quickly for fear of being caught out of position. This gives the offense an advantage.

Chapter Nine also discussed series and "alerts," which are two additional outstanding No-Huddle weapons. These tactics can change the momentum of a game or enable an offense to gain confidence at the beginning of a game or the second half.

The Appendix provides a troubleshooting guide to help a coach who is just starting to use this style of offense. This guide includes information that can help prevent problems from occurring or solve problems when they do occur. The problems listed in this guide are some of the most common problems that occur in the first few years of running the No-Huddle.

TO THE READER

Many of the following quotes have been inspirational to me in my quest for improved offensive performance and success. After each quote, I have included my own interpretation and application of that quote.

> "Has any man obtained inner harmony by simply reading about the experiences of others? Not since the world began has it ever happened. Each man must go through the fire himself."
> —Norman Douglass

Take the risk and try the No-Huddle. Mistakes can happen, but it is well worth the risk to improve your offensive production. We must all take a chance and pursue our dreams without fear of failure.

> "The quality of a person's life is in direct proportion to his commitment to excellence, regardless of his chosen field of endeavor."
> —Vince Lombardi

Coaches should always look for new and creative ways to improve their knowledge, experiences, and abilities. You should strive to improve and learn each day. Work to become the best possible version of yourself.

> "Genius is one per cent inspiration and ninety-nine per cent perspiration."
> "I knew 1800 ways not to make a light bulb"
> —Thomas Edison

Many times a coach must persevere to be successful. The first idea for executing a play may not be the best, but it might be a stepping stone to even greater ideas. Think about how the game of football has progressed over the past thirty years and the advancements made in the game. Don't look at failing as an end, but rather as a means to an end. Learn from your mistakes and failures to become experienced and educated about future possibilities. In the immortal words of Winston Churchill, "Never, never, never give up."

> "Even if you are on the right track, you will get run over if you just sit there."
> —Will Rogers

You must progress in this game or you will be defeated. Staying on the cutting edge of the game can have a dramatic effect on your success. The game continues to progress. Even though football is basically broken down into running, passing, catching, blocking, and tackling, many methods have been invented to improve the game. Everything from equipment and facilities to methods of weight and speed training have influenced the game of football. Continue to increase your knowledge, experience, and love for the game.

> "He was the sort of man who would go after Moby Dick with a row boat, a harpoon, and a jar of tartar sauce."
>
> —*Source Unknown*

This quote is all about attitude. It talks about a person who believes he will get the job done. When you set out to go for it, believe that the job will get done. The No-Huddle is a risky venture, but you must believe that you will figure it out and get it done. Your attitude can truly change every area of your life. Develop an attitude like the man after Moby Dick.

> "Almost all really new ideas have a certain aspect of foolishness when they are first produced."
>
> —*Alfred North Whitehead*

To be creative, you will usually have to look like a fool first. Christopher Columbus was viewed a fool to think that the world was round. To come up with creative ideas, you run the risk of looking foolish. Go for it. The No-Huddle might seem like a crazy idea, but it is really an effective tool in gaining an offensive advantage.

> "It is not what the coaches know that counts, but rather what the players have learned."
>
> —*Amos Alonzo Stagg*

One of the greatest football coaches of all time believed that the players are what make the difference in a team's success. As coaches, we may know a great deal about football, but unless we can communicate the information to our players in such a way that they can instantly retrieve it in a game, it is an exercise in futility.

> "If we did the things we are capable of doing we would literally astound ourselves."
>
> —*Thomas Edison*

High school players are very capable of handling the No-Huddle communication system. Coaches sometimes underestimate the mental capabilities of their players. Take the risk and challenge your players. People liked to be challenged. Believe in your system and in your players; it will pay big dividends.

> "Nothing great will ever be achieved without great men and men are great only if they are determined to be so."
> —*Charles De Gaulle*

To be great, you must desire to be great and to take risks in trying to improve your abilities to become a great coach. Be determined to be great and challenge your players to become great.

The No-Huddle offense can be run at any level with any offensive scheme. This book has focused upon different types of No-Huddle systems and how they can be run in a game. With this information, a coach should be able to utilize the No-Huddle to help elevate his team's offensive production and be more successful. Go for it.

No-Huddle Trouble Shooting

Even the best-built offensive systems can have some breakdowns. This appendix was designed to help prevent some problems from occurring and provide practical solutions when problems do arise. The following troubleshooting guide was designed to give coaches easy access to solutions for the most common problems that could develop in a No-Huddle style. My staff and I had to address these problems when San Clemente High School first went to this style. Although this list is not all-inclusive, it should enhance the implementation of the No-Huddle.

PRACTICE PROBLEMS	SOLUTION(S)
"Coaching" slows tempo in team periods	→ Must coach on the run. → Pull athletes out to coach and insert new player in team period while coaching. → Coaches maintain notes on mistakes to be discussed with players after practice. → All play adjustments must be made before or after practice as a coaching staff.
Practice tempo is too slow	→ Work on tempo in practice more. → Don't script plays. → Plan your tempos within practice. → Checklist the plays.
Offense fatigues quickly	→ Run more Up tempo in practice. → Have intense conditioning periods. → Develop goal of being the best-conditioned team in your league.
Some important plays don't get practiced	→ Develop "play checklists" for each period. → Structure down/distance "play checklists."

Defensive scout team can't maintain tempo	→ Teach scout team on Monday the defensive scheme for that week.
	→ Have two coaches running scout team (one for the front seven and dogs and the other for blitzes and coverage adjustments).
	→ Keep defensive terminology the same on both sides of the ball for easier alignment and adjustments. *Note*: This solution also helps with two-way players' defensive terminology retention.

GAME PROBLEMS   SOLUTION(S)

Game tempo too slow	→ More Up-tempo practice time.
	→ Simplify Up-tempo game.
	→ Before game, discuss with officials your style, tempo and game plan.
	→ Make sure the "chain gang" is aware of tempo (definite advantage at home).
	→ At away games, prompt officials to hurry the "chain gang."

| Teams disguising coverages | → Up tempo them. |

| Offense not effective | → Run a "series" for a momentum changer. |

| Ball boys not keeping up | → Carefully select 2-3 athletic ball boys who can stay focused for an entire game. |

Up tempo is too slow	→ Simplify Up-tempo game.
	→ Run one formation in Up tempo.
	→ Package plays on a wristband.
	→ Run high percentage plays.
	→ No check-with-me's in this tempo.

| Coach signaling in the wrong motion or play | → Have a smart quarterback who can make the correct call. |
| | → Find a new coach (unless it is you), but remember, mistakes can happen. |

Delay of games	→ Be focused when changing from Up tempo to Regular tempo (Officials are maintaining the same pace as before). → Make blitz adjustments basic and easily identifiable (i.e. limit the quarterback's options in unusual circumstances).
Series doesn't run smoothly	→ Must practice for 5 minutes each day → Practice Up-tempo pace. → Go on first sound. → All plays should be high percentage plays.
Defenses not aligning	→ Get the offensive line in their stance and the quarterback under the center. → Up tempo.
Penalty	→ Receivers must be within 15 yards when the ball is chopped into play.
Defense stems often	→ Up tempo to get them to align more quickly.
Two-way players can't get game adjustments	→ Huddle at the beginning of each series to communicate game adjustments.
Skill players run the wrong play	→ Require all skill players to watch coach signal in plays. → Coach should signal in every play in practice. → Randomly question resting players about what the play is immediately following the coach's signal.

COMMUNICATION PROBLEMS	**SOLUTION(S)**
Players can't hear play	→ Quarterback must cup his hands over his mouth when calling plays out. → Skill players should already know the play after watching the coach signal. → Use non-verbal signals.

Teams are picking up your signals/terms	→ Use dummy signals.
	→ Have two people signal in plays.
	→ Plays used most often should have at least two ways to call them.
Similar No-Huddle terms cause confusion	→ Use terms with 1-2 syllables.
	→ Terms must differ phonetically.
Players can't remember terms	→ Have terms with close associations to their meaning (i.e., terms start with the same letter as the play name).
	→ Test more often.
	→ Categorize terms according to category of offensive play (i.e., runs, passes, screens, etc.).
Regular tempo signals are slow	→ Quarterback looks away after motion signal and does not watch for play signal against teams that play a base defense.
	→ Receivers do not align quickly enough for the coach to identify the defensive scheme.
Line calls can't be made	→ In Up tempo, plays should not all require line calls.
	→ Line calls are made immediately following the play call.

Mark McElroy began his football coaching career in 1983 as an assistant to Allie Schaff at San Clemente High School. From 1983 to 1987 he coached a variety of positions for the Tritons. After earning two master's degrees, he left San Clemente to pursue his doctorate and coach football at Brigham Young University. In 1988 and 1989, McElroy was the head junior varsity coach and the running backs coach under LaVell Edwards. The Cougars went 19-7 in those two years and in 1989 won the Western Athletic Conference Championship. In 1990, after completing his doctorate in sport leadership at BYU, McElroy moved on to Whitworth College in Spokane, Washington. At Whitworth, he served as an assistant professor of physical education and the coach of the defensive secondary. He helped guide the Bucs to a record of 6-3, their best since 1975.

In 1992, McElroy returned to San Clemente High School as the head football coach. The team had not won a league game in the six years prior to his arrival. The Tritons are now a yearly playoff contender in CIF Division I, the most difficult high school football division in southern California. In 1995, San Clemente went 8-2 and defeated Mater Dei (the defending *USA Today* National Champion), snapping the Monarchs' 41-game winning streak to win the South Coast League Championship.

In the past five years, San Clemente has produced 13 Division I-A athletes. Under McElroy's tutelage, four of San Clemente's five quarterbacks have been 1st team All-League selections. All five are playing college football, three on Division I-A scholarships.

After careful research and contemplation, the football staff at San Clemente High School installed the No-Huddle offense in 1994. The first year was a learning year, and the team averaged just 23.5 points per game. Since then, however, McElroy has guided his offense to two successive 4,000-yard 10-game seasons while averaging over 30 points per game. During these two years, McElroy produced two different quarterbacks who each threw for over 2,500 yards and were rated among the top five at their position in Orange County. His teams have also included two different receivers who each had 1,000-yard seasons and were 1st team All-County selections, and a running back who compiled over 1,000 rushing yards in both 1995 and 1996.

Currently, McElroy teaches physical education at San Clemente High School. He is also a graduate faculty professor at Azusa Pacific University, where he teaches graduate classes in physical education and athletics. He has spoken at many football clinics and authored several articles, and is sought after as a speaker at churches, retreats and local service organizations. He is also a member of numerous professional organizations, including the AFCA and Fellowship of Christian Athletes. He runs a FCA huddle group at his home.

He is happily married to his lovely wife, Deanne, and they have four children: Seth, Caleb, Hannah and Grace. They live in San Clemente and really enjoy spending time together at the beach.